"In this beautiful book, Anna Woofenden tells the story not just of a new church, but of a new kind of church. If you are close to giving up on the church, or if you, like Anna, feel an irrepressible seed of hope for the church growing in you, this is the book you've been waiting for. When you come to this sentence late in the book, you'll dare to believe that it is actually true: 'God is making church all over the place, beyond the walls, on the streets, in the soil, and around the table.' And even more—you'll want to be part of the buzzing, colorful, nourishing garden that God is growing wherever there are willing gardeners to join in the fun."

—**BRIAN D. MCLAREN**, speaker, activist, and author of *The Great Spiritual Migration*

"The story of the Garden Church is a story about redemption, new imagination, and embracing abundance. Anna Woofenden boldly sketches a personal story, not shying away from the realities of life in community and the intense challenges of the pastoral vocation, but offering a vision of expansive community where we all can come in our brokenness to be healed. If you are longing for a new vision for what 'the church' can be, read this story of hope and courage and let the hope for beloved community grow and flower in you."

—**AMY BUTLER**, public theologian and former senior minister of the Riverside Church

"This book is a gift for those longing to hear how to restore the streets, rebuild the ruins, repair the breach, and raise up the foundations of a new church. The Garden Church is like a spring whose water does not fail. It is rowdy and elegant, ancient and new, difficult and true."

—**SARA MILES**, author of *Take This Bread* and founder and founder and director of The Food Pantry

"People often ask me how to get millennials to come back to church. Many of the answers are right here in this book—we have to be willing to reimagine church, literally from the ground up, giving place to imagination and holy risk-taking. As Anna Woofenden's gorgeous memoir makes clear, it's both challenging and hopeful to sift through the compost heap of the inherited Christian tradition to find what will, with God's help, spring forth into new life."

—**JANA RIESS**, author of *Flunking Sainthood* and *The Next Mormons*

"Planting a sustainable new church can seem like an impossible task, yet Anna Woofenden accomplished it with an empty lot and a dinosaur sculpture. Then Woofenden infused *This Is God's Table* with her wisdom, showing us the practical steps without hiding the struggles. This book is a beautiful glimpse into the hard and generous work of growing a church, a garden, and a community."

—**CAROL HOWARD MERRITT**, pastor and author of *Healing Spiritual Wounds*

"In a time when the church seems marked more by 'We've never done it this way before' than by 'We can dare to take chances with God's love,' Anna Woofenden delivers a book that tells an important story about taking chances. Everyone who reads *This Is God's Table*—especially those who care about the future of congregational life—will discover that there really is enough right under our feet to make church together, and that God is already blessing our wildest ideas about the church."

—**PAUL D. FROMBERG**, rector of St. Gregory of Nyssa Episcopal Church

"Tired of 'This is what the church used to be' stories? Does your imagination of what church can be need a new lens? Then *This Is God's Table* is the book you need. Anna Woofenden offers readers a riveting account of what it means to lead a new church movement with conviction, vulnerability, and most of all, hope. We all have much to learn from her."

—**ELIZABETH HAGAN**, pastor and author of *Birthed* and *Brave Church*

"In *This Is God's Table*, Anna Woofenden joins God at work by sowing kindness, planting gardens, and growing an unconventional church on a vacant lot. Profoundly lovely, wise, challenging, and grace-haunted, it is a story every pastor, congregant, and Christian should read to discover what it might look like to 'seek the peace of the city' and end up forever transformed."

—**COURTNEY ELLIS**, pastor, speaker, and author of *Almost Holy Mama* and *Uncluttered*

"With stunning clarity and refreshing humility, Anna Woofenden reminds us that 'God is making church all over the place.' Woofenden chronicles the gestation, birth, and growth in grace of the Garden Church with poignancy, honesty, and generosity of spirit. Her pastoral wisdom reminds us that even in the face of scarcity, there is always enough as the people of God persist in a 'heavenly way of being' on earth. This book will nourish your soul and till the soil of your imagination to envision the church in a fresh, life-giving way."

—**STEPHANIE LOBDELL**, campus pastor at Mount Vernon Nazarene University and author of *Signs of Life*

"At once a memoir and an ethnography, a story and a sermon. Through the lens of this small but mighty garden church, Anna Woofenden advances the tradition of Christian innovation while elucidating God's enduring care and relevance for us all. A joyful ministry about which to read!"

—**HARRISON BLUM**, director of religious and spiritual life at Amherst College

"When Anna Woofenden felt God's prompting to plant a church, she didn't necessarily expect actual planting to be involved. But down on her knees, with hands in the dirt, she faithfully tended both crops and a congregation to life. *This Is God's Table* shares the story not just of the Garden Church, but of a community strengthened together through its hunger. It tells the story of a town where all—whether pastor or parishioner, housed or homeless, longtime resident or new to town—learn to feed and be fed, thanks to an unassuming plot of land and the power of the Holy Spirit."

—**KENDALL VANDERSLICE**, author of *We Will Feast*

THIS IS GOD'S TABLE

THIS is GOD'S tABLE

FiNDING CHURCH BEYOND the WALLS

ANNa WOOFENdEN

foreword by SaRA mILES

HERALD
P R E S S

Harrisonburg, Virginia

Herald Press
PO Box 866, Harrisonburg, Virginia 22803
www.HeraldPress.com

Library of Congress Cataloging-in-Publication Data
Names: Woofenden, Anna, author.
Title: This is God's table : finding church beyond the walls / Anna
  Woofenden.
Description: Harrisonburg, Virginia : Herald Press, 2020. | Includes
  bibliographical references.
Identifiers: LCCN 2019045481 (print) | LCCN 2019045482 (ebook) | ISBN
  9781513804835 (paperback) | ISBN 9781513804842 (hardcover) | ISBN
  9781513804859 (ebook)
Subjects: LCSH: Garden Church (San Pedro, Los Angeles, Calif.)--History. |
  San Pedro (Los Angeles, Calif.)--Church history. | Church.
Classification: LCC BX8741.S26 W66 2020 (print) | LCC BX8741.S26 (ebook)
  | DDC 277.94/94083--dc23
LC record available at https://lccn.loc.gov/2019045481
LC ebook record available at https://lccn.loc.gov/2019045482

THIS IS GOD'S TABLE
© 2020 by Herald Press, Harrisonburg, Virginia 22803. 800-245-7894.
    All rights reserved.
Library of Congress Control Number: 2019045482
International Standard Book Number: 978-1-5138-0483-5 (paperback);
    978-1-5138-0484-2 (hardcover); 978-1-5138-0485-9 (ebook)
Printed in United States of America
Cover design by Reuben Graham

Portions of chapters 3, 7, and 10 appeared in the January 16, 2019, issue of *Christian Century* and are used here with permission. Portions of chapter 8 appeared in *Brethren Life and Thought* 62, no. 2 (Fall/Winter 2017–18), and are used here with permission.

24 23 22 21 20   10 9 8 7 6 5 4 3 2 1

FOR EVERYONE WHO
BROUGHT THE GARDEN
CHURCH TO LIFE:
THANK YOU FOR SHOWING
ME WHAT CHURCH CAN BE.

CONTENTS

FOREWORD

If you pour yourself out for the hungry
and satisfy the desire of the afflicted,
then shall your light rise in the darkness
and your gloom be as the noonday.
And the Lord will guide you continually
and satisfy your desire in scorched places
and make your bones strong;
and you shall be like a watered garden,
like a spring of water,
whose waters do not fail.
And your ancient ruins shall be rebuilt;
you shall raise up the foundations of many generations;
you shall be called the repairer of the breach,
the restorer of streets to dwell in.
—Isaiah 58:10-12 (ESV)

Those who take up the work of connecting faith with food—and with gardens, for that matter—can find a great deal of support in Scripture. The Bible's abundant images of milk and honey, figs and olive trees, bread and wine, oil and cool water nourish our faith and remind us, like the first garden, of God's presence and love.

But what the Bible also vividly describes is God's presence and love made manifest in the bodies of the lost and sick and humiliated, in crowded city marketplaces, in fights among neighbors and struggles over money, in the prayers of an afflicted woman and the songs of hungry people far from home.

And this is the gift of the Garden Church, and the gift of Anna Woofenden's tender and exact book: to show it all, and to help us move closer to wholeness.

There was a woman named Anna, sent from God. She was not herself the light; she came to bear witness to the light. Alone, she crammed her little Honda full of pots and pans and books and gardening tools, found a cheap apartment in a run-down Southern California port city, rented an empty lot, tucked her hair behind her ears, and began to figure out the call. People ignored her. "I don't even *get* San Pedro," Anna told me, in one of her earliest and most prophet-like rants. "Why here? Who am I supposed to be talking to?"

Luckily, since Anna didn't know who she was supposed to talk to, she talked to everyone. And since she didn't know exactly what she was supposed to do, she did it outdoors, building a garden where everyone could see. Anna was determined to open the gates to everyone who could possibly be hungering and thirsting for righteousness in San Pedro: the young Chicano barber, the cranky old Croatian lady, the shady real estate agent, the hopeless drunk, the afflicted single mother. She was meticulous about signs: centering the tree trunk as altar, creating the tender opening and closing of each liturgy, measuring the pace of silence and seasons, setting the table, trusting the sacraments. She poured herself out, feeding every-one who showed up, giving each the work they needed and asking all to break bread together, to pray for one another, to dig in the dirt and pull weeds side by side. And in God's own unpredictable, herky-jerky time, these strangers became a people, growing toward the light.

With wisdom and honesty, Anna has written it all down: this book is a gift for those longing to hear how to restore the streets, rebuild the ruins, repair the breach, and raise up the founda-tions of a new church. The Garden Church is like a spring whose water does not fail. It is rowdy and elegant, ancient and new, difficult and true. The call, Anna discovered, was "simply what my grandparents and great-grandparents were called to as well: to discover what it means to be faithful in our gener-ation, for this season, in this garden." She has planted in faith. May the work of her hands, and of the whole Garden Church, be witness to the light.

—SARA MILES is an author whose books include *Take This Bread, Jesus Freak*, and *City of God*. She served as director of ministry at St. Gregory of Nyssa Episcopal Church in San Francisco for ten years and is the founder and director of The Food Pantry.

AUTHOR'S NOTE

This book is the story of a community. In its pages are the stories of many people gathering to make church together. Each person in this narrative is precious, even though I can only give a tiny snapshot of them. While I sought to do each person justice, know that what you are reading is only a slice of the wholeness of who they are. Names and identifying details have been changed for some, and pseudonyms given for others. I condensed and rearranged the timeline for the sake of the narrative. I used field notes, emails, and my own memory to write these stories and in some cases was able to confirm individuals' direct quotes. In all, this is a story from one person's perspective. So many people were integral in the work of this church. My pastor heart wants to name them all, but my writer brain doesn't want to overwhelm the plot. Know that while many are not mentioned in this book in detail, each person I had the honor of making church together with is written in the soil of the Garden Church and its story.

-1-

THE TABLE

The oil sizzled as I poured it over the surface of the cedar stump table sitting in the May sun.

"We consecrate this table with the anointing of oil," I said as I continued pouring. "The oil that runs over the heads of those who are prophets and priests of God's message in the world. We anoint our table—the center of our worship space and our life together—with oil as it bears God's prophetic message to the world. This is God's table. All are welcome here."

Our unlikely group was standing in the middle of an empty lot in old-town San Pedro, a neighborhood nestled in the southern outskirts of Los Angeles. On either side of us were the brick walls of neighboring buildings. Along the back of the lot, a sagging fence separated the space from a public parking lot. A green fence, accented with wrought-iron grape leaves, opened to the street out front.

Just a few hours before, in my jeans and black clerical-collared shirt, I had walked out of the landlord's office with the code to the fence's padlock and the key for the water spigot. The office manager had given them to me nonchalantly; she had no idea what a monumental moment it was.

I was about to open the gates of the Garden Church for the first time.

Farmer Lara, a local master gardener I had been working with over the past months, walked to the site with me. We turned the numbers to the code on the padlock, opened the gates, and walked onto our lot—ours for the next six months, at least. It was a plot of littered, hard-packed, scruffy dirt contaminated by years of parked cars and city waste. All we saw was potential and possibility.

This was where the urban farm and outdoor sanctuary I had dreamed of for years would have its start. We were going to reimagine church here as we worked together, worshiped together, and ate together with all kinds of people. We would grow food, establish community, and connect with nature, God, and each other. This was it. Today was the day.

Farmer Lara, with her big straw hat to protect her from the California sun, and I got to work. We stretched a carpenter's measuring tape across the fifty-foot-wide plot, bringing to life the pencil sketches from my journal and the plans that Lara and her husband, Scott, and I had worked on around their kitchen table. We found the middle of the central circle we had envisioned and rolled the cedar stump over to it, scraping the ground so the stump would rest level.

When I had gone to the garden center earlier that morning to pick up the stump, the man who cut it and sold it to me had asked, "What are you going to do with this, ma'am?"

As the words came out of my mouth, I knew they were unexpected and perhaps a bit odd. "I'm starting a church that's in a garden, a garden that is a church."

"Wait. So, the church is, like . . . outside?"

"Exactly," I said with a smile, curious what he was thinking.

"So this stump is, like, church furniture . . . well now, that will be neat," he said.

"Yup, come down and see it anytime," I replied. "We'll be in the empty lot on 6th Street across the street and a bit down from the Warner Grand Theatre."

Karen had shown up as we were setting the stump in place. She had parked a few blocks away where the parking was free and slowly made her way with a cooler rolling behind her, filled with ice she had been making in her freezer all week. I first met Karen at Wayfarers Chapel, our sister church up the hill in the next town over, when I was on a scouting mission to see if Los Angeles could be the place to plant the Garden Church. After preaching at Wayfarers about this wild idea of a church in a garden and a garden in a church, Karen had come up to me after worship and said, "I see it, I really see it." When I arrived in August to bring the dream to life, she was one of the first people to seek me out, press a generous check into my hand, and say, "It's to grow the Garden Church."

We'd met a few times over the fall, and she continued to pray for the work—and ask the hard questions. "Is it really okay to be meeting in public parks, and do you know how rough that area of town is?" "How will it be funded?" "Do you really just move here and start this so quickly?" We talked through my research and my unanswered questions. I was open about the anxiety that comes from starting a church from scratch. Karen was the perfect foil. I had the vision, but needed to know more about the heart of the community. And even though that vision may have been outside Karen's comfort zone, she had a heart for the community.

Karen began coming to gatherings and worship as soon as we started. She showed up as we picked up trash in parks, planted lettuce seeds in pots to take home for our own dispersed garden, worshiped under a park tree, and learned to integrate the sounds of birds, sirens, and wind into the liturgy. We ate together, too—everything from peanut butter and jelly sandwiches that Karen brought to the park to the big pots of soup that I made in my small kitchen as we gathered in my apartment to dream and plan and pray. Karen was part of setting the tone in those early months: her heart was open and she was willing to *try*, to learn, and to faithfully pray daily for God's guidance in this experiment of faith as we took the church beyond the walls.

"Look at this place!" she said as she began plopping ice into cups and pouring the juice she'd brought for each of us. "It doesn't look like much now, but I can see it, Reverend Anna, I can see it—this will be God's church."

I got the rolled-up sign from the car and Farmer Lara held it up on the front gate while I attached it with zip ties. With each tie, we secured ourselves a bit more to 6th Street. The sign read:

Pop Up Garden and Gathering Space

A Collaboration between the
Garden Church and Green Girl Farms

Reimagining church as we work together,
worship together, and eat together.

We hung the sign not realizing we were providing a blank canvas for graffiti to come. For now, it was crisp and new.

Even as we hung it up, we began to make good on our hope that the "location, location, location" investment of renting this space was going to pay for itself in marketing. Right away, people walking by paused to ask what we were doing. We chatted with them, and Karen handed out postcards, sharing what we were doing and inviting people to join us. We attached a postcard holder to the front gate, and a week later, the first hundred cards were gone. People were curious about new activity in a lot that had previously been home to a few parked cars, sometimes a Christmas tree sale or beer fest, and always the faithful Dino.

Yes, that's right: a dinosaur. The lot was almost empty when we began renting it, but not quite. A twelve-foot-tall, garishly green, metal dinosaur stood in the corner. Years before, the lot had held all sorts of large creature statues for sale. After the sale was over, Dino remained. Over time, the lot became identified as the "Dino lot," or sometimes "Jurassic Park." Children and adults alike stood outside the fence, longing to say hello or get a photo with Dino.

The group of people who had been overseeing and giving birth to our church plant over the past fourteen months spent twenty minutes of the April board meeting deliberating whether Dino would stay or go. It certainly did not fit our hope for the decor, and it took up valuable growing space. Yet Dino was a fixture of the community we were joining. We decided to embrace the local, quirky nature of the predicament, and claimed Dino as part of our sanctuary. When asked about Dino in the months and years to come, we would say, "Dino was here before we were, so we let it stay. Look, we planted Dino its very own garden, and converted Dino from a carnivore to a herbivore!" Now that the gates were open, kids could run in and look up at the towering form. Teenagers came in to get selfies, and we chatted with adults who wanted to talk about the connections they saw between religion and science. Dino would become our ambassador, an icon in our space.

Our sign was up. Our gates were open. I felt too excited to focus, but the lot was ours now and there was much to get done that day. As we worked, Farmer Lara and I noticed how many people were coming by. Our street, 6th Street, held the weekly farmers' market. People were hanging out, picking up lunch and produce. The sound of live music drifted down the street. We decided then and there we would be open *every* Friday during the market to welcome people into the space. I didn't know how exactly this would work; I just knew the gates needed to be open whenever there was a flow of people on the sidewalk.

After our initial setup was complete, we had gathered around the cedar stump for a time of blessing. I watched the oil I'd poured on the table soak into the freshly hewn wood. Above the chatter of the shoppers at the produce stand outside the gate, I lifted my hands and prayed:

> As we open our gates, we ask you, O Lord, to watch over our going out and our coming in from this time forth, and forevermore. May everyone who enters here feel your love and the love of the beloved community. May this be a space of refuge and sanctuary, delight and abundance, honoring God and peace. Alleluia. Amen.

> At our center, we consecrate the table, the table that holds the symbols of our life together:

> The Bible, the Word of God, for the people of God.

> The candle, the light of Christ and the light in all people.

The water of life that nourishes and renews.

The bread that feeds us and the cup that reconciles us.

And the icon of the tree of life. Reminding us of why we are here—to cultivate a little more heavenly way of being, right here in the dirt of the earth.

People poked their heads in, wondering what was going on. I smiled and waved as we sang "Alleluia" together. With each refrain, we became more and more of a church, a sacred sanctuary, in the middle of the city.

My voice caught as I poured the rest of the oil over the table. Years of calling, wonder, hard work, and a *hope* that this wild idea could be realized were culminating in this moment. This was the beginning of the church I had dreamed of pastoring. "This is God's table," I repeated. "Where all are welcome, to feed and be fed."

Farmer Lara poured out parsley seeds saved from her husband's grandmother's garden. As they scattered over the table, Lara voiced the remembrance of those who had come before us and put their faith in our efforts and our hope to grow something wonderful for the future. We committed ourselves to the new seeds we would plant and nurture here.

Beside the stump we had placed a rosemary bush in a big pot. Rosemary is traditionally for remembrance—the perfect companion for the communion table, where Christ calls us to celebrate and share the bread and the cup and to "do this in remembrance of me" (Luke 22:19). Those of us gathered around the table took sprigs from the rosemary bush and dipped them in the water of the baptismal bowl, shaking the water toward each corner of the lot. We asked God's blessing, and dedicated the lot as sacred space—a place where people could find hope, a table where everyone could find belonging. We named it as a church, a spiritual community dedicated to loving God and loving each other together and being faithful, here and now, in our generation.

We were gathering in a centuries-old gesture of wanting to be a church together, but we were committing to doing it in a new way. It was not our intent to eschew tradition, yet we knew many traditional churches weren't serving some people and were completely missing others. We prayed that the people who would never walk through the doors of a traditional church might find a home here at the Garden Church. After years of longing, wondering, and planning what it might look like to reimagine church in this way, here I was, in my new city, bringing it to life.

The church has adapted from age to age to serve people in their local contexts. Monasteries, medieval beguines, prayer meetings, Catholic Worker communities—all were new ideas once. Innovative expressions of Christian community were, and are, part of a loyal response to God's call to faithfulness. As the Garden Church moved from dream into dirt, people, and plants, I saw it as just one expression in a long lineage of contextually creative responses to being church together. As a church planter, I felt the temptation, and even pressure, to be the new thing that everyone could follow, thus saving the dying church, but God and the wise faithful continued to bring me back to earth. My job was the same as the generations of leaders and communities that have been reimagining church in their own time and place. My job was to ask, How can we come together with others who are looking to be faithful in our generation? How do we be church, here and now, in our current cultural context?

The growing national trends around church and church-going loomed large over the work of the Garden Church. Or, rather, the trends around *not* churchgoing. The number of *nones* (those who claim no religious affiliation) and *dones* (those who once identified as religious but no longer do) in North America is growing.[1] It is not as simple as stating that "people just don't like church anymore." People cite not feeling welcome, the hypocrisy they see in religious traditions, and lack of engagement with the needs of the community and world around them. They say they practice their faith in other ways, but struggle with the idea of church. While many people have no interest in engaging in spiritual community, others are still searching for a place where they can connect in ways that nourish themselves and their families. And communities still long for the sacred and for church to be woven into the cracks and crevices and needs of the community.

This is a story about the changing landscape of church, culture, and community. It is the story of our efforts to engage faith, food, and neighbors in ways that would enliven and transform us, rather than divide us. And it is a story of the challenges, tears, friendships, and love that arose in the process. We gathered around God's table in an empty lot, and a church sprang up.

My calling to give this wild idea a try flowed from a central tenet: God is everywhere and moving in all things, and God is right here, present with us. So wherever we named and claimed God's expansive love and welcome, it would be church.

I didn't anoint the cedar stump, our table, with frankincense oil that morning in the empty lot on 6th Street because I thought something magical would happen. I anointed it because we humans need physical things to remind us of what is deeply true. In biblical texts and Christian history, the practice of anointing with oil is usually reserved for priests, kings, prophets, and leaders—anointing gives them permission to lead, to proclaim, to be prophetic witnesses. On that particular Friday, we did not pour oil over my head or Farmer Lara's. Instead, we poured it over the table. The table would be a place that we would continue to gather around. It would prophesy the deep truth that all are welcome around God's table. It would be the magnet that drew us together, the old friend that reminded us why we belonged, the symbol that radiated God's love.

After I gave the very first benediction in our outdoor sanctuary, I opened a bag of almonds and apricots that I had stuffed in my purse while running out the door early that morning, and we ate together. TeaJ and Nancy walked into our outdoor sanctuary. TeaJ carried a watering can, gardening gloves, and a gift certificate to Home Depot. Nancy held a folder with some newspaper clippings and names of people I needed to connect with in the neighborhood. I had first met TeaJ and Nancy over a year before when I was scouting out the area as a possible place to plant the church. The embodiment of deep faith and hospitality, TeaJ had invited me to stay for ten days in a studio apartment in the housing complex she helped manage while I researched the area. We sat in her cozy living room, and I shared the vision of creating a place where all different kinds of people could come together and be welcome, a place where we could eat together and get to know our neighbors.

"Honey," she had said, "that's just what church should be." She described the potlucks at the church of her childhood, and her belief that God guides and provides in the everyday things of life.

TeaJ stayed to help welcome people in as they came through the gates to see Dino and ask what we were doing with this empty lot. I walked out to canvas the neighborhood with postcards and introduce the church. The others stayed back to continue cleaning up, bending to pick up broken glass and pull dry weeds from the packed gravel.

As I returned through the gates, I saw people moving and working around the cedar stump that we had consecrated. I felt my breath quicken. This was a moment of arrival, the first of many that would come in the life of this church becoming a church. After months of planning, fundraising, wondering, hoping, doubting, and believing, here finally was our chance to see: What happens if you plant a church that is a garden and a garden that is a church? Who would gather around this table, God's table, where all were welcome?

-2-
ROOTS

I spent much of my life longing for a church where I felt fully welcome.

The Garden Church is the main character of this book, and in these pages you will meet many of the people who nurtured, tended, and grew it alongside me. It has been my privilege and my work to plant this church, and now to tell the story of how it grew. Its origins are mingled with the soil of my own life. How we ended up on the hard-packed dirt of that Los Angeles lot has much to do with my own search for a church to be part of and to serve.

I grew up on a homestead on an island in Washington state. There I played with and helped care for my six younger siblings—as eldest children in large families often do. I climbed trees, planted radishes and forget-me-nots in my own little garden bed, and built forts shaded by a big Douglas fir and old-growth cedar trees. I worked in the family garden as well,

helping grow vegetables to add to the steady stream of grocer-
ies needed to keep us all fed.

Living close to the land gave me many gifts, but at times it
was also hard and lonely. Being homeschooled, coming from a
large family, and living on an island a short ferry ride from the
larger town set me apart. Wearing thrift store clothes and not
having cool new toys added to my differences. I now appreciate that my parents encouraged us to read, make art, and play
outdoors instead of watch television; at the time, I couldn't
keep up with conversations with my peers about *Full House*
or the latest music video.

And then there was our religious heritage. We were part of
the Swedenborgian Church—a statement that throughout my
life has generally elicited the response, "Sweden-what?" As a
child, I didn't know the depth of my family's extended history
with this small Christian movement, nor have any idea that I
would one day be ordained as a minister in one of the branches
of the Swedenborgian Church. I only knew that because we
were a part of this particular religious path, we didn't go to
the church down the road, and we spoke of faith and God in
different ways than some of my friends. Like many of you,
no doubt, I have a complex religious family background. But
I didn't know I was not alone in that complexity; at the time,
I felt I was the only one who didn't quite belong.

Both of my parents grew up in the Swedenborgian faith,
although in divergent branches of the denomination, one more
liberal and the other more conservative in theology and social
norms. My father's family moved around the States until his
father settled outside Boston for a long tenure as a professor
at the Swedenborg School of Religion, the denominational
seminary of the more liberal branch of the Swedenborgian

tree. My grandmother, a brilliant theologian and scholar in her own right—although women in her day were not called theologians—had a minister father and a theologian mother. She raised eight children, developed Sunday school programing for the entire denomination, read New Testament Greek while knitting, and planted gardens at every house they inhabited.

My mother's family moved frequently and attended Swedenborgian churches where they could. My grandparents eventually settled on an island in Lake Michigan, where they became integral to the local ecumenical community church and tended a huge vegetable garden and a flock of chickens near their small cabin.

My parents met at a Swedenborgian college outside Philadelphia. They married in 1978. When spring came, they headed west in their 1965 VW bus with visions of finding a homestead, growing their own food, and putting down roots close to the land. They ended up on an island in the Puget Sound in northwest Washington.

A long two hours from our island homestead was a Swedenborgian church in Seattle. When I was young we made the drive there most Sundays. As we drove south, passing the church on our island and the many evangelical and mainline churches across the channel in town, it was reinforced to me that our branch of Christianity must be unique if we were making such an effort to worship there and not with our neighbors.

As I look back now from a more ecumenical perspective, it is perhaps surprising that my parents made such an effort in those years to connect with the tradition they were raised in. Why not worship on the island with our neighbors? The Swedenborgian culture was our family lineage, the church we were taught to have allegiance to, even when across the country and far from the familiar. Being part of it, even in some small way, connected us to our extended family and the tradition they were dedicated to.

But one Sunday we didn't pile into the old VW and make the drive to Seattle. No one told me why. Years later my parents would talk about the complicated struggle to feel part of the community, since we only attended once a week, along with the practical difficulty of the trip as our family grew in size. At the time, I only knew that I missed the music, lighting the candles, playing with friends, and rolling down the big grassy hill during coffee hour. Most people have never heard of the Swedenborgian Church, but as a six-year-old, it was the only church I really knew.

The Swedenborgian Church originated in a pub in London in the late 1700s when a group of men, mostly clergy, together read the theological works of an eighteenth-century Swedish theologian and mystic, Emanuel Swedenborg. Some read Swedenborg's theology as research for their Sunday sermons in their Anglican churches. They were drawn to his concept of a layered reading of the Bible, his vivid descriptions of life after death, and his unusual acceptance of various religious paths. Another group took Swedenborg's vision of a "new Christianity" as a call to start a new denomination. They were Baptists and Methodists, street preachers and reformers, eager to start a movement. This latter group began training and ordaining clergy and establishing churches. The seeds of their vision crossed the ocean and took root in North America, where they founded what is now named the Swedenborgian Church of North America in Philadelphia in 1817.

As a nation established in part on freedom of religion, the young American republic was awash in a sea of religious movements and groups (albeit most of them Christian). Within this context, many Americans felt empowered to leave existing religious communities and join new ones, especially communities that emphasized direct religious experiences. Methodists, Baptists, Mormons, Disciples, and Shakers were all groups who, in varied ways, said that God was still speaking to people, especially ordinary folks. And these groups grew at astounding rates in the first decades of the nineteenth century.

In Philadelphia, the Swedenborgian tree flourished in this fertile soil. After a few generations, a branch split off, people who craved a new life apart in an intentional religious community. They moved to a wooded hill on the outskirts of Philadelphia to create a utopian community and schools exclusively for children in the church. My maternal grandmother would be born in this town, where she would make her way through the tree-lined paths up to the Gothic-style cathedral on the hill for worship every Sunday. Later, my parents would walk these same paths while attending the college where they met.

After we stopped going to the church in Seattle regularly, we began having family worship at home instead. We pulled chairs into a circle, sang, read from the Bible, and said the Lord's Prayer. I always wanted to be involved, and my leadership skills began to emerge as I shared how I thought worship should go. It was sweet to gather as a family in this way, but my world had suddenly gotten smaller, and I missed our church community.

I found joy in working in our big garden. I found peace and curiosity playing in the woods, building forts, and climbing trees with my siblings. This nurtured me. But while I didn't have the words for it at the time, looking back I see signs of my longing for a consistent spiritual community. I longed for others with whom I could freely ask my questions about God and do Sunday school lessons. I missed those home-baked cookies at coffee hour. We sometimes gathered with other dispersed Swedenborgians in the greater area around the holidays or when a guest minister from out of town would visit. Sometimes we'd make the trek to the Swedenborgian family camp in the Northwest, or to the camp in Maine that my father's grandparents had founded.

Then, as a preteen, I started to rebel against my parents by going with my friends to the evangelical youth group in town. My parents were glad to see me finding community, but uncomfortable with the accompanying theology. I, however, was discovering the intimacy of prayer, and I began going to the Bible regularly to hear God's voice. We had weekend retreats and weekly discipleship groups. I was told that people were proud of me and grateful for my contributions. I was empowered to lead. As a teenager, this sense of being part of something was paramount.

Yet this was not the full answer to my desire for belonging. I could never completely relax within this community. At the time, I fell in line with the evangelical moral and cultural norms, but the theology stung and chafed. I embraced the people, but kept my background and questions under wraps. If I wanted to belong, I needed to belong on their terms:

theologically, morally, and culturally. I always watched myself. I was on edge. For my youth pastors, there was only one way to God and heaven; unless you proclaimed Christ in a particular way, you were damned to hell. Yet at home, I was taught about a God who welcomed all different kinds of people into heaven, and that it was both our belief *and* the way we lived that mattered.

I was leading a double theological life. It seemed the only way to survive. The evangelical church was my friend group and my community. But I felt sure—and I may have been absolutely right—that I would no longer be accepted if I were honest about my questions, my theological concerns, and my heart-of-heart knowing and beliefs. My God was different from their God. I had no place to put this truth. With a Swedenborgian backdrop behind me and the church of my teenage years not the answer either, the tension between my worlds grew.

Throughout high school, I felt a hunger to learn more about the Swedenborgian theology of my family tree. I applied to the same college my parents had attended. At eighteen, I arrived there with an open heart and quickly soaked up theology classes, all-college worship, and conversations over meals at the dining hall. I was so excited to be around people with whom I could talk openly about my love for Swedenborgian concepts. I led Bible studies and worked on church outreach. My calling to ministry began to sprout. Like my grandparents, aunts, and uncles before me, I was called to the life of faith and exploring theology with others.

But as this path unfolded, I began feeling constraints. I spotted signs I had somehow failed to notice along the way: the lack of women in spiritual leadership; the socially conservative, sheltered, and restrictive culture. Just as I had felt in my youth pastor's living room during Bible study with my friends, I began to wonder if there was enough room for my questions and for what I thought I might have to offer my church.

A few years after college graduation, I got my dream job as an outreach director at a church in Boulder, Colorado. Although the church was part of the same conservative branch of the denomination, it was committed to doing church in new and welcoming ways. If there was going to be a place for me in this denomination, this church was it.

In Colorado, I bought a townhouse, dug out the landscaping rocks in my little square of yard outside the front door, and planted a garden to see what I could grow. I dove into my new role. As I grew, my call to ministry grew as well. I loved being present with people in pastoral care situations and found I had a good sense for welcoming people into a community, removing barriers, and leading small groups. I discovered my ability to help create and cast a vision for what church could be. I found home and community nestled near the Rocky Mountains.

But I was drawn to activities beyond the scope of my non-ordained role: engaging deeply with theological study and teaching, preaching, leading worship, and presiding over the sacraments. I was finally forced by my own inner truth to question my belonging in an organization where I, as a woman, could not be ordained. My job description hadn't narrowed; my call was widening.

The questions that surfaced were not just about my own sense of what God was leading me toward. I was also wrestling with questions like, What is the church anyway? How can we speak of spiritual nourishment when there are empty stomachs sitting in our pews? Where do justice and mercy fit in? These questions were the early etchings of a church, a spiritual community, a ministry to which God was calling me.

The call became louder, and the need to move on from my congregation and denomination became clearer. I wanted to pursue ordained ministry. God's message, "Go therefore and make disciples of all nations" (Matthew 28:19), kept appearing in front of me, until all I could hear was "*Go.*"

I transferred my membership to the more progressive and inclusive branch of the Swedenborgian family tree and applied for the ordination track in the Swedenborgian Church of North America. From the outside, this might seem like an easy transition to have made—leaving one Swedenborgian community for another—but the divide between them was notable. As someone with heritage in both, I had felt the animosity between the two branches my whole life. In leaving one and going to the other, there was loss and the feeling of betrayal. I also found connection and new beginnings—I was preparing to follow in the footsteps of so many of my father's relatives. People recognized my last name; they recalled taking classes from my grandfather, or were reading my great-grandmother's books of biblical exegesis. This community welcomed me with open arms. Here, my gender was no longer a barrier to my calling. I also suddenly found myself among Swedenborgians who engaged and existed within a larger ecumenical world. As I pursued a degree and ordination, I was encouraged to explore and see how this tradition fit within the history and movement of the broader Christian family tree.

Sojourning with the Quakers, I earned my Master of Divinity at the Earlham School of Religion. I studied at the Center for Swedenborgian Studies in Berkeley, surrounded by a plethora of traditions in the Graduate Theological Union. I washed feet and explored ritual and preaching with the Church of the Brethren. I spent a summer in Washington, D.C., with an ecumenical cohort of Beatitudes Society fellows, and worked at the faith-based food justice advocacy organization Bread for the World. I did field work at St. Gregory of Nyssa Episcopal Church and The Food Pantry in San Francisco. I went to a church planters' conference where most of the speakers were women, from all over the denominational spectrum, showing me that this could be my story. My world widened. My appreciation for the many and varied branches of the Christian tree grew.

I began to feel more and more at home, drawing on a variety of traditions to flesh out what it looked like to be the body of Christ. The things that divide us—exactly how to preside over the table, membership, baptism, theological particularity—seemed less and less important to me. The Episcopalians taught me the power and depth of liturgy and the centrality of the eucharist, holy communion. The Quakers taught me the power of silence and the importance of contemplation and action in the work of justice and peacemaking. The Brethren lifted up the priesthood of all believers. The Lutherans gifted me with seeing the power of a church planter who could create a community around her explorations of the Lutheran theology that everyone is simultaneously sinner and saint. My Presbyterian mentor showed me how the structure of the mainline church opens up a space for women to be ordained fully into leadership. I found myself identifying with the broader and varied progressive Christian movements, while centered in the Christian tradition of my ancestors, but now in a form expansive and inclusive of a variety of paths.

While a part of me felt like I never quite fit in anywhere completely—I still needed to explain *Swedenborgian* to the wider world—I was finding my way and feeling part of the body of Christ.

In each of these traditions I gravitated toward people who were asking questions about food and faith, ecology and theology. I studied how the sacrament of communion had been used to include and to exclude throughout history. I explored the work of Helen Keller—while she is perhaps most well-known for her humanitarian activism, including for the deaf and blind, she was also a devout Swedenborgian whose spirituality led her to works of justice and beauty as she connected with God and nature. I dedicated a seminary New Testament paper to exploring who might have been with Jesus at the Last Supper, making a case for a crew of disciples from varied walks of life that could have surrounded him. I took every chance I got to have communion and share a meal with a different religious group. The sacrament of breaking bread together at a table captured me wherever I was, giving me a moment of belonging.

As I sojourned through school, trainings, and internship placements, I tried to plant at least a few pots on the back stoop of every place I lived, if not a whole garden. I kept an eager eye out for growing space in cities and towns. I found something sacred in seeing how nature persists in urban environments and I always looked for ways to grow more food in proximity to those who were going to eat it.

And I sought out church planters and people who were experimenting with church in new ways. I made my way to the

House for All Sinners and Saints in Denver and to St. Lydia's, a dinner church in Brooklyn. I met with founding pastors and read every book, social media post, and website I could get my hands on that explored church planting and doing church in creative ways.

The vision began to sharpen. Food. Community. Sacrament and prayer and singing. People fed in body, fed mentally and emotionally, fed in spirit. I do not remember the exact day the idea for the Garden Church took shape, but what I do remember is sitting across from a seminary professor at a coffee shop and saying, "What if everyone got their hands dirty? What if we had church in a garden, where we grew our own food?"

It was during seminary that I also began to understand better the multilayered factors that lead to poverty, hunger, and inequality in general. It became clear to me that starting a new and interesting church was not enough—I wanted the church to have a focus in the community that would contribute to a more just and generous world, rising out of a dedication to being a community of faith. I envisioned not just a church without walls, but a church that would engage other faith groups in the work beyond the walls and in the community.

Growing up in a rural environment, where poverty often is not as visible as in urban communities, I did not have much experience with people living on the streets. I remember visiting "the big city," Seattle, and seeing people on the sidewalk with signs asking for money. Having no context for their need, I felt uncomfortable and not sure what to do. Even while volunteering at a local shelter in Boulder, getting church people together to work at the food bank, and striving to educate myself on the issues in the region, some part of me still held the people I encountered at a distance. I was thrown off by the unpredictability. I kept getting caught up in the need to fix things and despair that I couldn't make everything better. And beneath that, I was hindered and protected by my own privilege. In learning more about the worlds of my neighbors, the differences in our realities sharpened.

When I moved to Berkeley to finish seminary and do field placement at the Food Pantry and St. Gregory of Nyssa Episcopal Church, something new happened: I got to know people whose life story included living on the streets or couch surfing from a friend's apartment to a neighbor's shed.

The Food Pantry is a pop-up farmers' market that forms weekly around the communion table in the middle of St. Gregory's ornate sanctuary. It was founded by Sara Miles, a writer and visionary, as her response to the eucharist, at a table where "all are welcome without exception." Being part of this community blew open the doors to my ideas of how church could encounter people from different walks of life. The Food Pantry held a big, unwieldy community where people were loved and fed. Here, the people who came for food stayed to help, working side by side with volunteers like me. Taya had a thick Russian accent and gave bad dating advice. Margo, who presided over the bread table, ensured that no one took more than their share. I broke down boxes in the back parking lot with José, and watched Tom gruffly manage the line of people waiting outside.

"You gotta be strict with them, but you know I love 'em," he said with a wink.

The Food Pantry moved my heart and mind, helping me sift through what I could give—food, prayer, resources, support—and what I couldn't: a house, medication, easy solutions, lives restored to what they had once been. Walking through the San Francisco streets felt different to me after my time in the Food Pantry community. I was challenged to see the image of God in each person I encountered.

During my time at St. Gregory's, I was finishing up my last seminary classes, and I knew that this idea to plant a church needed practical attention if it were to become a reality. I talked to denominational leaders and church planters. I quickly narrowed my vision to the West Coast, as the region's Swedenborgian denominational body was open to and supportive of new initiatives. Then I began to look at cities up and down the West Coast. I wanted to be somewhat near a large, stable, and supportive Swedenborgian church, which narrowed it down further to somewhere around San Francisco or Los Angeles.

When I said to people in San Francisco, "I want to plant a church that's a garden and a garden that's a church," I heard responses like "That's cool, that reminds me of . . ." They would go on to tell me about an amazing urban farm or a creative church they had been part of. In Los Angeles, the response was, "That sounds cool, I want to be a part of it." I took this as an affirmation of the work I hoped to do, and decided to go to LA. But once my heart and mind settled on LA, I still faced greater discernment. I read about the region's demographics and area churches. I looked up community gardens and farming projects. I spent ten days exploring the cracks and crevices of the area, all the while praying, "Show me, God, show me." The decision felt both crystal clear and arbitrary; while so many neighborhoods stood out, it was San Pedro, a neighborhood filled with beauty, possibility, struggle, and need, that called to me.

I once traveled to England with my friend Jana, who would later become an integral founding board member of the Garden Church. During the trip she and I spent a day with an Anglican priest in Sheffield in northern England.

"I'm going to show you my parish," he said that morning. American Protestants that we were, we expected that he would show us his church building. Instead, he pulled out a map and traced the boundaries of the portion of town that was his to care for. He drove us by the elementary school where he had led morning worship a bit earlier, by the retirement community where he did pastoral care, past the jail where he visited inmates, past the sports fields where he cheered his people on. His responsibility, he explained, was not just to the people who showed up at the church on Sunday morning, but to all those living in his area, and to the community as a whole.

Like a mayor of the soul, I thought.

When it was time to launch the Garden Church, I wanted to live out the English priest's model in our context, of being the pastor to the neighborhood, not just the people in my congregation. I wanted to create a place where *all* could come together and reconnect to their food, to the earth, to each other, and to God.

I had the support of my denomination, the Swedenborgian Church of North America, and the encouragement of many across the country who were praying and contributing in many ways. The support and encouragement allowed me to take this leap of faith, but I knew I needed people on the ground. So, before I knew enough people in LA to have a local board, we established a start-up board. Jane, Jennifer, Amy, and Rebecca flew in from around the country for a long weekend of meetings. Jana made her way through the congested LA traffic. Katherine and Emma, whom I barely knew but who were introduced to me by trusted friends, said yes when asked if they wanted to be involved in this wild new idea.

During our weekend start-up board retreat, we walked the streets of San Pedro and talked to people. The wealthier people I had talked to in Palos Verdes, the affluent neighborhood up the hill, had told me about San Pedro. "Gangs, drugs, and homeless people," someone said. Others used words like *unsafe*, *rough*, and *surly* to describe the area. Yet, as I got to know my new town, I saw so much more. Words like *beauty*, *resilient*, *tradition*, *hardworking*, *culture*, and *pain* felt more accurate. Clearly, one of my hurdles—and my opportunity— was to create a space where those from up the hill and those down in Pedro could meet, mix, and get to know one another.

I began to invite people like Karen to join me in walking the community. "This sounds good," she said at the end of a lunch together. "I am nervous about coming into that part of San Pedro—its roughness is out of my comfort zone—but I'll give it a try."

Nancy and Emma had lived in San Pedro for years and saw the rich beauty of the community in and among the broken places. We walked and prayed and asked about the needs and the gifts of the community. One might call it market research. One of my seminary mentors called it "exegeting the community." To me it felt like walking on holy ground. We walked by the empty lots, the grocery store, the elementary schools, and the tent cities. We saw the people God was weaving together in community. To be faithful to what the church is able to be in this generation, we recognized that we could not be set apart from the needs and gifts of the community around us. We had to be embedded in the systems and relationships that were there. And I, being new to the area, knew that my first and most important job was to listen.

I knew we were not going to solve huge systemic issues with a church plant. I was committed, however, to doing my best to be aware of them and to be curious how this start-up church might play a part in a movement toward equity and justice: in access to food and community, in ways for unhoused people to be known by housed people, in using empty lots in urban environments to grow food.

The food system continued to rise to the top as I talked to people about where there was access to food, fresh produce, and hot meals. The more I learned the more complicated I realized it was. Physical access to the food was not the only factor; racial discrimination, classism, and economics were integral as well. I looked for the teaching of others who were working at the intersection of these issues around the country. In the eastern United States, my friend and colleague Rev. Dr. Heber Brown founded the Black Church Food Security Network in response to what he calls "food apartheid": the ways that policies and racist systems are constructed to limit and control people's access to food. "Communities struggle not just with access to healthy food," he says, "but because they don't have control of their food system."[1]

In San Pedro we found a few grocery stores, but mainly dollar stores and small markets that didn't carry any fresh produce. We talked to people and learned about the residents of a low-income housing building. Their small community garden was packed with people, many of them immigrants, growing produce they had grown in Guatemala, Vietnam, and Chile, and cooking dishes that their grandmothers cooked. There was a waiting list to get a garden spot, and the desire to have more growing space in the community was high. I fluctuated between inspiration and being overwhelmed as the needs and the possibilities became clearer, as we grew in awareness of our new neighborhood.

During our explorations of San Pedro's streets, we kept coming back to an empty lot in the middle of 6th Street. It was in the old-town district, an area that those up the hill might come to, with shops and art galleries and twinkle lights woven above the streets. Maybe in this contested, overlapping space people could encounter each other and start to see neighbors as human, not as each other's issue. Yet 6th Street was in a twenty-block area considered by some to be rough. The rental agent, the man at the deli, and some people from the church up the hill cautioned me that as a single white woman, I would not be safe living there. The neighborhood held a mix of people: some owned their homes and were barely holding on to them thanks to high housing prices and taxes. Many lived in low-income housing; a few lived in the couple of nice apartment buildings with gates and codes; and some lived in the park, in their cars, and on the street.

As we walked the streets and had worship in various parks around the community, these particular neighborhoods became my parish. I was being called to pastor not just the people who attended one of our gatherings, but also the ones who lived in the alley, who worked at the mechanic's shop, the family living in their car, and the wealthy patron who wanted to clean up the block. Somewhere in these twenty blocks was where we needed to plant the church. If this was where people were hungry, if this was where people were in need of being fed in body and mind and spirit, if this was where the middle- and upper-class people on the hill wouldn't come at night, then this was exactly where we were being called to create a sanctuary, to plant the church.

Walking by the empty lot, Dino watching us from behind the fence, the vision took on specific angles and shades. I saw garden beds and a compost pile; folks from up the hill and just around the corner; an open gate, a table, and a group of people gathered around it. At long last, it was time to put down roots and plant a church where any and all could belong.

-3-

WHERE ALL
ARE WELCOME

Welcoming all people around God's table is easy to say, and much harder to do.

When we placed that cedar stump table in the middle of the empty lot, we were claiming geography that was engulfed in a long-standing San Pedro conflict between the people living in houses and the people living on the streets. Local business owners on 6th Street loved that we were cleaning up the filthy lot and planting flowers; they weren't so sure about the people we were welcoming through the gates.

Within the first week of being on 6th Street, a business manager a few doors down offered to let us use their bathroom facilities. I was thrilled. "An answer to prayers!" I happily texted our board members. "The manager is even willing to leave the back door open so we can enter and exit without disturbing the customers."

This worked well until one of our congregants, who traveled with her backpack and all her belongings, went over to use the bathroom, alongside a well-dressed mom with her young child. This prompted the manager to speak to me in hushed tones, rescinding the offer. "We can't have all the homeless people on the block using our restroom," the manager said with a shake of their head.

I called an emergency board meeting later that day, we approved a line in the budget, and we had a porta-potty delivered to the lot by the weekend. However tight our budget was, whatever resources we had at the Garden Church needed to be shared and available to everyone—including the unhoused members of our community.

"All are welcome" was a value we repeated over and over at the Garden Church. We wrestled with it as we looked for the image of God in all people, in everyone who walked through the gates. This endeavor was an ongoing challenge and blessing, both personally and collectively. The phenomenon of group "othering" was alive and well in the community. As theologian James Alison puts it, "Give people a common enemy and you will give them a common identity." We sought the wisdom of Alison's follow-up: "Deprive them of an enemy and you will deprive them of the crutch by which they know who they are."[1] In those first days as we built garden beds, shoveled soil, and put the rainbow tomato cages in the circular garden around the sanctuary area, I was reminded of my own tendency to ignore or brush off people with whom I didn't know how to engage. Sure, I didn't think of them as my enemy, but I certainly struggled daily to not think of them as being "other" than me. I knew our call was to move *toward* those seen as "them" or "other," yet it was not always clear to me how I could serve and connect with our neighbors who came through the gates pushing shopping carts or carrying all their belongings on their backs.

Soon after the gates of the Garden Church opened, Denyse saw the sign and postcards on the front gate and came in, wearing faded yellow overalls, a pink sweatshirt tied around her waist, and a big backpack with a bedroll attached to the side of it on her back. She entered quietly during worship and sat down. She offered a quiet prayer request during prayer time, and her eyes lit up when I said, lifting up the bread and cup during communion, "All you need, to eat here, is to be hungry."

"Yes, please," she said when Karen offered her a bowl of soup during dinner time. After everyone had eaten, there was still minestrone soup left in the vat I had made.

"Would you like to take this with you?" I cheerfully offered, gesturing at the pot.

She looked at me directly, patiently, and said, "It's really nice of you to offer me the leftover soup, but I don't have a safe place to put the pot, so I would have to carry it around with me all week until I saw you again next Sunday."

My gut twisted. How could I be so stupid and insensitive? Of course she couldn't carry my pot around and return it clean, with a nice thank you note tucked inside. She didn't have a home, a kitchen, or any storage space to call her own.

In those first weeks, Denyse taught me much about being unhoused. If I was going to pastor this community, I needed to be a quick study in the realities of my parishioners' lives. I had to look beyond the solely spiritual needs that presented themselves in worship and consider systems, needs, and resources within the community as a whole. I had so much to learn.

Denyse had entered the gates and shown up ready to live our tagline, "Feed and be fed." She showed us what she was hungry for—physical food and nurturing community—and what she had to offer—agricultural and artistic experience, faith, wisdom, connection. She said she would love to tend to plants and that *yes*, she would like to come back during the week and help in the garden. On Tuesday, Denyse dove right into planting tomatoes and beans with Farmer Lara. On Friday, Denyse came back again as we opened the gates, right on time and ready to do whatever was needed. Denyse, Stephanie, and I began building the benches for the sanctuary out of four-by-four beams and stacked and glued cinder blocks, using a pattern that Stephanie had found on Pinterest. Stephanie had joined us after hearing about our efforts at Wayfarers Chapel and had been getting more and more involved. She had generously arranged to have the supplies delivered from Home Depot earlier that day. When we finished the first bench, Denyse looked up and said, "I helped make something. That feels good."

Then, on one of our first Fridays that the Garden was open, I watched a grandmother in her pressed white pants observing Denyse carefully chalking the word *welcome* on our sandwich board sign. The woman approached me, "I've always thought those homeless people couldn't do anything useful, but look at her, she's doing such a beautiful job on the sign!" My muscles tensed. I froze my face lest my judgment show.

I spoke the truth, not just to make a point but because it was the reality. "Yes," I said. "Denyse is an important part of our community."

The growing group of folks who were showing up at the garden and striving to be a church together saw that it was not just about Sundays. We wanted to be a place where all are welcome to feed and be fed, all the time, not just on Sunday afternoons when we had our weekly gatherings, where we worked, worshiped, and ate together. We wanted to have our gates open as often as possible—certainly whenever something was happening on the block. Every Friday we opened for the hours that the street was shut down for the farmers' market and welcomed people in as they looked around at the tiny sprouts popping up in the garden beds and asked, "Wait, what is this? A garden or a church?"

"Both," we would reply, and go on to describe this place where we were committed to feeding in body, mind, and spirit.

People kept coming and going and poking their heads in through the gates whenever we were open, wondering what was happening in the "Dino lot."

One Friday morning, an older man drove his pickup truck to the back gate with a picnic table from a neighborhood family. They had used the long, red table and its accompanying benches for years for family meals outside. But their children were grown now and they were ready to pass it along. And their good friend obliged their need to transport it.

"Rev, I've got something for you," he called over the sagging gate.

"Come on in!" I called to him, walking over to undo the padlock. We unloaded the table together, then the benches, and then it seemed like he didn't want to leave.

"I'm not so sure about religion," he finally said. He went on to tell me about the ways he had been hurt by the church, and how he didn't see it as necessarily a positive force in the world. I listened, sympathizing with the all too familiar stories. "But this place," he reflected slowly, "I can feel the love here; I can feel God."

One evening a month, the downtown area hosted a First Thursday art walk. The blocks around us were filled with food trucks, open shops, and galleries. Our second month on 6th Street, my sister Nora, who had just moved to the area, put together an opening musical set and recruited a new friend, a lawyer-turned-musician who was trying to make it in the LA music scene. Farmer Lara, her husband Scott, and I strung solar-powered lights above the space, rented a small generator to power the sound system, put on our name tags, and opened the gates. To our great surprise and delight, people came. Stalwart Karen, Nancy, and Stephanie showed up. They donned the burlap and blue jean aprons that Stephanie had made for the volunteers and helped greet people, hand out postcards, and answer questions.

A mother and daughter who had started coming regularly on Sundays and Fridays came in halfway through Nora's set. The daughter was eight and had just starting homeschooling, and her mother used the garden as a classroom. Our youngest consistent volunteer, she became integrated into our work, especially the managing of the farm stand. We had a table with whatever veggies we had available, supplemented by Farmer Lara's other gardens, and fruit from neighbors' trees. A large sign on the table read, "Take what you need, pay what you can," and the produce was feeding a growing number of people. On this Thursday evening, our young farm stand manager was ready. "We've got basil and radishes and kale!" she called out to people as they walked by the table near the front gate.

A week after our first art walk event, a member of a friend's local church came to help at a Friday gardening time. I remembered that she had been deep in conversation during the evening music as she sat on the benches in the sanctuary with a friend, burgers in hand from one of the local food trucks. I was happy to see her in the garden again, helping children plant seeds.

When they left, she came up to me. "Can I talk to you for a minute?" she asked. We sat down on a bench by the prayer garden. She reached for my hand and pressed a big rainbow-colored marble into my palm. "I want this to be somewhere at the Garden Church," she said. "As a thank you for being a safe and welcoming space. Because last Thursday, after the music, I came out for the first time. This space was a safe place for me to have that conversation and feel the support that is proclaimed at the table."

I had tears in my eyes as I held up the rainbow marble and saw it with the rainbow tomato cages in the background. "We'll put it right here in the prayer garden," I said, "as a sign and a covenant of God's love and welcome."

One Sunday evening, I walked by the food table while Denyse and Karen were busy packing up leftover lasagna and rolls. Denyse took them up to the homeless camp nearby, but returned a half hour later because a few rolls were left over. She wanted to make sure that someone who needed them took them home, and she wanted to return the canvas bag. She reported how appreciated the food was. "If you haven't been actually hungry for a few days, you don't know how good food can taste. It's important for people to be fed," she went on, "because all those people, they're human, they deserve to be seen. In my tradition," she continued, "we say, 'Food is God.'"

The next week, Denyse and I had a long conversation about gardening and homelessness, and she described herself as a bridge between the communities. She mentioned that some of her friends who live on the streets might really benefit from getting their hands in the dirt.

"I don't know if you'd consider having a 'homeless' garden?" she asked.

"Well, this is it!" I said. "Everyone is welcome here. Especially those who don't have their own homes and gardens to work in."

But the look on her face told me I wasn't listening. She looked around at the kids who were happily playing in the dirt and running carefree around the space. "I don't know . . . some of my homeless friends are a little rough," she said, pondering whether they would mix with the explorative toddlers.

I realized she was actually wiser about these dynamics; her realism tempered my aspirational idealism. We began to talk about Friday gardening time and how we could create culture and values in the space so various members of the community could feel safe and welcome. We talked about finding a way that everyone would be welcome whenever the gates were open, but how we could focus different times more specifically for different facets of the community. And that while we wanted all people to be welcome, not all behaviors would be welcome if we were going to be a hospitable space for everyone.

"All people are welcome, but not all behaviors are welcome" was a guideline I'd learned from my friend and mentor Sara Miles while working at the Food Pantry in San Francisco. But as I was still learning, saying it was easier than implementing it.

Before I had even unlocked the gates one Friday morning, one of our neighbors from the barbershop found me in the parking lot to tell me something. "There were homeless kids smoking and hanging out in the garden yesterday, and I think they may have slept there," he said. Then another neighbor came over from across the street to tell me the same, and a bit later, a third. My heart pounded as I thanked them for letting me know, and told them that when we were there and the gates were open, all people were welcome, but when the gates were closed, it was a private space. I gave them my phone number in case they needed to get in touch in the future. I felt vulnerable and exposed; things were happening in our space when I wasn't there. I asked for a description of the young people who had been there. I knew who they were.

It was a trio of young people, including one named Brayden, who had been to the garden a lot recently. Brayden had contributed significantly to the gardening process, and I was excited to have him involved. They had been coming more and more and getting more comfortable there. Perhaps too comfortable, I thought.

When Brayden walked through the gates on Sunday afternoon I felt my stomach drop. How could I welcome him *and*
make the boundaries clear? "All people are welcome, not all
behaviors are welcome. All people are welcome, not all behaviors are welcome," I repeated to myself as I took a deep breath
and sent up a prayer for help in navigating this conversation.
I watched from the other side of the lot as Farmer Lara welcomed him and put him to work turning the compost. After a
few minutes, I walked over to say hello.

Brayden stayed through worship and shared some Scriptures that were important to him during the sermon response
time. Then, later during the meal, I heard the squeal of the
back gate being opened. Brayden walked over and brought a
couple of guys in. I shook their hands and welcomed them to
the Garden Church and invited them to come eat. One of them
stayed after dinner and participated in closing circle, the final
part of our worship service.

Brayden remained after the service, and I knew I couldn't
avoid the conversation any longer. He sat on a blanket near the
altar as I packed things up. He told me of his struggles with
faith and feeling on the outside of the community, not knowing how to trust the people around him. I felt torn between
affirmative pastoral listening, the need to state the boundaries
of the space, and my own desire to avoid unnecessary conflict
with a community member.

I finally got it out. "I want to make sure you and I are clear
about your connection with this community, Brayden," I said.
"You and everyone else are welcome at the Garden Church
when the gates are open and the staff is here. And when the
gates are closed and the staff isn't here, no one should be in
the garden. This is for the safety and liability of everyone." We

were still working to find the line between private and public space; having a staff person present any time the gates were open was our best plan at that point.

Then Brayden told me he had seen people in the garden hanging out on Friday morning. "I jumped the fence to tell them to leave and help them clean up," he said.

I decided to go with it. "Thank you, thank you for helping to hold this space and respect it and share the boundaries."

I felt him saying what he wished were true. He said he had told the others to come back during the day on Fridays or Sundays, so I knew that he knew the boundaries, even if he hadn't followed them.

A few minutes later, after we finished packing up, I went over to Brayden and asked, "Hey, by the way, can you take your stuff with you this evening?" I pointed to a skateboard and other items that were lodged in the corner by the back fence. "I'm really sorry, but we can't store it here."

"It's not mine. I don't have a skateboard," he said. I raised my eyebrows and decided to give him an out.

"Hmm . . . well, it can't stay here, so I'm going to put it outside the gate. If you know anyone whose it might be, could you see that it gets back to them and let them know that they can't store it here?" I pulled out a big bag, the skateboard, and a tarp and handed them to him over the fence.

"Huh, that does look like homeless stuff," he said. I didn't say anything more other than to thank him for helping find the owners.

I didn't know it then, but Brayden wouldn't come back after that. I saw him here and there around town and waved hello, but as much as I had tried to make clear that he was welcome, after naming the boundary that he could not camp out and sleep in the garden, he drifted away. I struggled with wanting to be able to serve everyone and be the safe place where he could find the support he needed. His withdrawal felt like a failure on my part, and I wondered if I could have done better.

After speaking with Brayden that evening, I went home to my empty apartment and flopped on the couch. I opened my laptop to email my friend and mentor Sara, in San Francisco. I knew she would understand the messy exhaustion of trying to welcome all people while also needing to have boundaries and supporting people who showed up.

> I'm so, so tired, Sara. I know I would probably be bored in a "regular" congregation, but this is so hard. Church is messy, I know, and we can't serve everyone, and I can't fix all the issues in our community, as much as I would like to. And how the heck do we welcome everyone, but still keep boundaries?! I keep repeating what you always say at the pantry: "All people are welcome, but all behaviors are not welcome." But it's hard to explain this to someone who is desperately looking for a place to belong *and* needs a place to sleep at night. This tension tires and flattens me more than other things.

> I need to shower and try to relax. That was one hard week. But I know this is just the stuff of this ministry work. I do believe that. This is the stuff of following Jesus and having a church that's willing to go there to follow Jesus.

> Thanks for witnessing.

> Love and oxox, Anna

The email swooshed off to Sara, and the words of Isaiah echoed in my ears:

> The Spirit of the Lord is upon me, for God has anointed me, God has sent me to bring good news to those who are

poor; to heal the brokenhearted and to proclaim release to those held captive . . . to comfort all who mourn, to give flowers instead of ashes . . . the oil of gladness instead of tears,

the cloak of praise instead of despair.

They will be known as trees of integrity, they will rebuild sites long devastated; they will repair the ruined cities . . .

For as the earth brings forth its shoots, and a garden brings its seeds to blossom, O Exalted God makes justice sprout, and praise spring up before all nations. (Isaiah 61:1-4, 11 TIB)

At the end of the service the next Sunday, I went over to Denyse, who had been working hard cleaning up the space.

"Denyse, you're awesome. Thanks for staying to the bitter end to get things put back together."

And she looked at me shyly and said, "Of course. This is my home."

I smiled. The fact that we couldn't be everything for everyone was feeling abundantly clear, but here was a distinct reminder that we could and were making a difference for some of the people coming through our gates. *Okay, God,* I thought to myself, *I guess we need to keep showing up.*

Instead of the fantasy congregation I'd envisioned for myself, I had a real live one: a fluid collection of some disenfranchised by the church, some faithful Catholics, and a whole bunch of unhoused neighbors with needs I couldn't even begin to meet, who were hungry and ready to participate. This was the church God was giving me to pastor. These were the poor, the brokenhearted, the captives. This is what had happened, in this time and place, when we said, "All are welcome."

This was who showed up. It was my job to keep showing up and opening the gates.

-4-
THERE IS ENOUGH

Every Sunday before our community meal, we would sing a blessing song together, "There is enough, there is enough, there is enough, enough and some to share." In a society so focused on consumption and scarcity, this was an essential mantra for our community—and for me.

As a pastor to a new community, I spent a lot of time worrying about whether there would be enough. Enough food for the community meal each week. Enough volunteers. Enough money in the bank account. Enough energy to work another long, hard day. Enough of me.

In the early weeks and months, I never knew who was going to show up and if we'd have a critical mass or not. If all we valued was attendance numbers, Memorial Day weekend worship the first spring we were open, for example, would have been dubbed a "failure." The few regulars we had were out of town. As we moved through the three movements of our Sunday gathering, we had five people for work time, seven by the end of worship, and eight in time for dinner. A combined attendance of eleven.

Is this even worth it? was the refrain running through my head.

Even though I knew I was not the only one keeping this thing going, it took constant reminders for me to believe I wasn't alone in the work.

It was in April, just before we opened our gates on 6th Street, that my sister Nora moved to the area. She was just out of college and was in LA to follow her music therapy career and forge a path in a new town. Nora dove into helping with the church, giving countless hours leading music for the worship service, being present, and generally making sure I did not crumble under the pressure of church planting. In those early days, sometimes Nora and Farmer Lara were the only people I knew for sure would be there on a Sunday afternoon.

One Sunday Nora and I were driving to church when she reminded me, "The Spirit seems to be pretty faithful, Anna. Maybe we can trust that she will blow in just the people we need."

"You're right," I said. "Maybe the Holy Spirit works collectively?"

"Yes, I think she's saying: 'I'll send you the help you need—it's just going to come from different people each time, and you may not know about them or know who it's going to be beforehand. It fact, you probably won't, so you have to trust me,'" Nora mused.

It seemed that our search for *enough* had as much to do with attentiveness to what was already there as it did with acquiring new things or people. *Enough* was about seeing how

God was *already* giving us what we needed, rather than wringing our hands and grasping for what was to come.

When preparing sermons I used the Revised Common Lectionary, a series of Scripture readings that progress chronologically through the Bible, mark sacred cycles throughout the calendar year, and are used by Christians around the globe. The first summer we worshiped together regularly was the season that many dub the "endless season of bread," because for five weeks in a row the gospel passages in the lectionary feature stories about bread: the bread of life, bread from heaven, and of course, the feeding of the five thousand using a few loaves and fish. In the text of the story from the gospel of John, the loaves and fish are provided by a young boy, and in the end there is so much food that there are leftovers. This gospel text showed up the same week a ten-year-old boy provided his own feeding miracle for us.

This feeding in the gospel story begins with Jesus seeing the people and acknowledging their hunger. Jesus knew that teaching hungry people ideas was not enough. The people whom Jesus fed were the outcasts and struggling of their day—people who had no power or influence, people who came because they were "sheep without a shepherd" (Mark 6:34). The disciples wanted to send them home, but Jesus was, as the text says, moved to "compassion." Or that's how the Greek word *splagxnízomai* used here is generally translated, but it's more visceral than that. The word also conveys that Jesus' heart went out to them—his insides, his guts, his very being saw the need on the face of humanity that he loved, and wanted to do something about it. But he did not just clap his hands three times and have food appear. He engaged a process with the disciples, with the hands and feet that were called to follow the Lord. The disciples thought the whole thing seemed impossible. "This is a deserted place, and the hour is now very late," they said; "send them away so that they may go into the surrounding country and villages and buy something for themselves to eat" (vv. 35-36).

Jesus replied, "You give them something to eat" (v. 37). In other words, "Feed them yourselves."

He asked how many loaves of bread they had. They responded, "Five, and two fish" (v. 38).

This passage cut to the heart of my perpetual internal dialogue as pastor of the Garden Church. Will there be enough food on Sunday? Are the volunteers going to get burned out? How will we do more fundraising? And those were just my worries about my little fledgling organization in this one corner of one city; I also worried about injustice, poverty, racism, corruption, and violence across the globe. Like the disciples, I found myself exclaiming, "Seriously, Jesus, can we please just send it all away?!"

Jesus asked his disciples, and kept asking me, to "bring me what you've got." I believed this to mean: Bring your talent and passion. Bring your broken places and the strength you've gained through hard times. Bring your fears and your vulnerabilities. Bring the five loaves of bread, the things you love. Bring those two fish, the things you know. Bring your brokenness and your wholeness. Bring them to me.

Jesus then blesses the "little" we have, the crumbs we have to offer. Jesus blesses the bread and fish, he blesses the loaf and cup, and one crisp fall afternoon, Jesus blesses the pesto chicken and the hands of a ten-year-old boy, who filled our bellies to bursting at the Garden Church.

The boy had come the week before to do volunteer hours for his fourth-grade class. We put him to work planting, weeding, and watering. He was obviously unimpressed, and politely made it clear it was not his favorite thing to do. I sat down with him and his mother to ask what things he liked to do. It turned out, in fact, that he loved to cook. "Well, that's a wonderful miracle!" I exclaimed. "We are in desperate need of more cooks for our Sunday meal!" His face lit up, and he shyly asked what needed to be done.

The next Sunday he came proudly in through the garden gates with his mom and another friend from his class. They each bore large dishes of breaded eggplant, pesto chicken, and a two-tiered carrot cake. "Come look, come look!" I called Nancy, Karen, and Stephanie over. "Look! It's our feeding miracle for the day!" Everyone oohed and ahhed over the food as the boys proudly explained the spices they had used and how they'd picked some of the veggies from the garden.

When the sermon was over that afternoon, we moved from communion—our sacred meal—to our community meal. The line around the serving table formed quickly. Some of the neighbors from the street jostled to the front. That day, no one held back. There was so much food, thanks to the boy and his willingness to offer what he had.

God kept showing up at the Garden Church to take the "little things"—the things that we might have deemed insignificant—and say, "Oh, yes, let's use that." Hanging out with Jesus was changing our relationship with what was *enough*. Despite our worries about a lack of money or big crowds, the Garden Church kept gathering, contributing, sharing, and working together.

It also pointed out to me places where scarcity and greed were at work in our society.

As I watched Betty shuffle in through the gate with all her possessions in her shopping cart and Chase pushing Marion in her wheelchair with their bedrolls hanging on the back, the needs of the world weighed heavily on my heart and mind. The repercussions of greed and capitalism, rapidly rising housing prices, and the lack of accessible healthcare were no longer abstract ideas to me. The more I traced the chaos and pain I saw coming through our gates, the more I saw how one could trace it back to the need to accumulate money and power, and the deepening of economic divides.

Showing up each week to make church together reminded me how we are all tied up in each other's well-being. As I heard the stories of poverty and struggle and pain, I found my own battles with scarcity and disbelief in *enough* being challenged and cracked. Coming around that table together each week meant that we were invited—sometimes compelled—to hear God's truth, the truth that combats scarcity, breaks down consumerism, and invites us to look honestly at our collective societal sins. And it was also around that table that we heard God's truth in the consistent assurance that "there is enough, there is enough, there is enough, enough and some to share."

I clung to that refrain, humming it over and over throughout the week. Despite my daily attempts at hope and a mindset of *enough*, I never knew who was there for a day, just for one service, and who would become a core member of the community. I constantly weighed how attached to get to people. For every ten people who came a few times and were so excited about getting involved, maybe one would be there six months later. I found my ego getting caught up in measuring my worth on whether the church plant was working or not. "Maybe I could have said something, done something, that would have made that person stay," I would think, inaccurately claiming for myself a level of power and influence over people's choices about how to spend their time. Humbled by this realization, I worked at staying present and appreciating who was there right then.

A good friend once told me, "I don't think there's such a thing as human unconditional love from one other person, but maybe in community, we can find it." This resonated with me, and I think it is why we need the community of church; in church, it is not just me as an individual who counts on another individual whose life, ability, and availability can change. Instead, it is us collectively counting on each other, and more than that, counting on God. And God was showing me to be less narrow-minded and much more creative about what the church I could count on might look like. As people showed up with what we needed to take the next step—be it in the form of a large check from a friend hundreds of miles away or a used cooler that showed up on the hottest day of the summer—the Garden Church was teaching me that the church was actually God's and not mine.

<center>~~~~~~~~~~</center>

I found myself on a weekly rollercoaster of beautiful miracle moments, and the depths of what felt like too many hard things. My spiritual muscles grew as I sang, "There is enough, there is enough, there is enough, enough and some to share" each week, as I began to see and believe in *enough*.

Until the next day, when I would forget. Every time the bank account started getting low, the uncertainty around the future loomed. I would forget that there was enough, and then we'd have our monthly board meeting via Skype and board members would step in, participate in fundraising efforts, and give generously themselves. We had funding from the denomination, some local people who were beginning to give, and over seventy-five people across the country who were giving in small and large amounts to help us get started. But it felt like the end of the funding might be just around the corner at any moment. As fall approached and our six-month lease was nearing its end, the board met to take a serious look at our finances. The big question hanging over us was: can we afford to keep renting the space?

"We have a very narrow margin," our treasurer pointed out, "and the rent is our second biggest expense after your salary and benefits." I sighed. The audacity it took to raise money for a new project was exhausting to me, and even more so when my own income and livelihood relied on it.

"The location has been our very best advertising," I said. Thanks to our greeters who stood at the gates with counters discreetly held in their hands, we knew that almost five thousand people had been through the gates in our first five months, mostly people who had come through on Fridays during the farmers' market, or during the monthly First Thursday art walks.

"The location is really key," Katherine chimed in. "My friends and neighbors here all know the block, and the dinosaur, and are curious about what's happening."

Jana added, "We're taking a leap of faith here, because we believe God is in this and good things are happening in this space. We need to ask our donors and community 'will you leap with us?'"

By the time Jane, our board chair, called for the vote, it was a unanimous *Yes* to negotiate for another year on the lease, with the heavy knowledge that we were stepping out on a limb. Trust was carrying us through; a whole lot of fundraising was ahead of us.

"There is money out there for good things," Jana reminded us. "And this is a good thing."

I grew into a comfortable routine of being in the garden, working from my home office, and being present out in the community. As we moved into our first fall, more people were committing and getting involved. Some part of me started to relax. I delegated more of the volunteer management and weekly tasks. In mid-October, someone committed to organizing the volunteers for food one Sunday, as well as put together gift baskets we were preparing to present to visiting donors at dinner. How incredible to have someone offer to help in this way.

Then, on Sunday afternoon as I was driving to church, I got a text saying that the volunteer in charge of food for the community meal that day was sick. Not only were they sick, they had been sick since Saturday morning and hadn't completed the gift baskets or arranged for anyone to bring food for the meal.

I just about blew a gasket. Why hadn't they called me yesterday morning when they first got sick? And why, when I'd asked if we were all set for volunteers, had they said yes?

I sat in the car and prayed for help. I prayed that I wouldn't bring the stress with me through the gates. I was angry and disappointed, and so, so tired. I kept taking deep breaths, willing myself not to leak anger out all over. Karen was there when I arrived, and dove right into setup. Farmer Lara came in a few minutes later and I let loose a quick rant, in hushed tones, into her confidential ears. I tried to push back the rush of thoughts this was bringing up for me, mostly: I need people I can count on.

Karen didn't know what was going on, but as she was setting up the worship space, I went over to her and put my arm around her and said something vague about needing to breathe and pray. She squeezed my waist with her soft arm and we stood in prayerful silence. I felt my heart open. Slightly.

I calmed down by the time worship started, but as I looked over those assembled for worship, I realized it was the smallest gathering since we had opened six months prior. I felt utterly deflated. On the spot, I changed the opening Scripture from my regular "This is the day that the Lord has made; let us rejoice and be glad in it" (Psalm 118:24) to "For where two or three are gathered in my name, I am there among them" (Matthew 18:20). I acknowledged how tough everyone was for coming out in the heat and in that busy season. I found myself apologizing for the fact that we were such a small group. I hated apologizing—it discounted the people who had shown up, I worried—but I also wanted to acknowledge my disappointment at the empty chairs.

I tried to redeem my defeated invocation by talking about how important it is to keep coming together and doing the liturgy together, even if there are just a few of us. Karen, Nancy, and Denyse nodded. Nora sang extra loud.

As we began sharing prayer requests, a few more people came in, including two young men who looked around curiously and then sat down when Nancy gestured for them to join us. As we chanted the communion prayers, the words of the gospel kept echoing in my ears. *Take, bless, break, share . . . Everyone was fed . . . And there were twelve basketfuls left over.* Just as we started communion, Sarah, Ed, and their toddler, Leia, walked through the gates. The three of them had started coming regularly. Leia and I had been bonding over watering cans and playing with Mono Verde, the green stuffed monkey that was her constant companion. Leia toddled up during communion, lifting her arms for me to pick her up. She snuggled up against me as I began to chant the prayers.

When it came time for dinner, Nancy saved the day by going out to get pizza.

Karen had magically left cookies before she headed home early. A young friend of Nora's showed up unexpectedly with eggnog. She poured glasses for everyone while we were waiting, and proclaimed with a smile, "Life's short, drink dessert first, pizza is on its way!"

We gathered back together for our closing time, and Leia came over to me again. I held her as I proclaimed the benediction blessing with her warm arms around my neck and an increasingly softened heart.

Yet again there had been enough. But was enough . . . enough?

Then, just a few months later, there was too much. Our regulars were slowly increasing, but most of them were hungry for community and church, not necessarily food. Denyse had invited some of her unhoused friends here and there, but with the transient nature of living outdoors, many hadn't kept coming. I was at a loss. How could I gently welcome more people who were hungry and experiencing homelessness while also being mindful of the capacity of volunteers who I feared might get burned out from bringing food?

One morning when I preached at Wayfarers Chapel, our nearby sister church, I met a recently retired engineer with a flair for the cuisine of his home country of France. He was looking for a hobby for the fall before he and his wife started traveling. I invited him to come visit the church.

He came by the next Friday and he and Farmer Lara quibbled over how to cut herbs as they harvested a couple of boxes of greens, basil, thyme, and zucchini. He planned on making a huge batch of food because I said we usually had around twenty to twenty-five people, which had been the average over the past month or so.

Then, on Sunday during worship, there were only nine of us—blame the football game, the film festival down the street, or the cool breeze . . . or perhaps church planting is just completely fickle and you never know if anyone is going to show up. Knowing that our French cook would soon show up at the gate, loaded with trays of food, I started to get anxious. It felt like every week was a test of whether this church, and my leadership, was succeeding—and that people were looking at attendance as the ultimate arbiter of this question. And now this friendly volunteer had gone to all this trouble to cook, wanting to give back to the community, and there was no way that nine of us were going to be able to do his meal justice. As we ended communion and were about to transition to dinner, I told the nine of us gathered what was up.

"Friends, our job tonight is to eat and appreciate this meal, but more than that, I need everyone's help thinking of people who are hungry, and we're going to pack it up and share it with those who might need dinner tonight. And let's pray for some people to come through the gates who are needing dinner right now and want to eat with us."

Immediately, voices started to buzz. One person said they could take food to someone who often comes to church and who was living outdoors nearby, another to their friend who was homebound. Another said he'd head up the street and invite people on intermission from the film festival to come down. By the time the food arrived, a small crowd had gathered.

As people came in, I asked them if they knew anyone else who needed dinner, and they went back out and invited their friends who were hanging out down the street. Randy, a guy who spent a lot of time at the local coffee shop, always wore a herringbone flat cap, and had started coming most Sundays for dinner, walked in. "Hey Randy, anyone else you know hungry? Will you ask them to come help us out? We really need more people to eat." He headed back out and soon returned with a group of people I'd been wanting us to invite, but hadn't quite connected with yet. They got plates and started talking with everyone. A mother and daughter who were at the film festival down the street came in to look around and get their picture with Dino. I invited them to stay and the mother politely said they couldn't—but I looked over a few minutes later and there they were, sitting at the picnic table and eating, because the daughter had insisted she was hungry *now* and wanted to eat with us.

More waves of people arrived. By the end of dinner, more than thirty people had been fed. "The biggest compliment to the cook is when everything is eaten," our proud cook stated. I was shaking my head at God, who always seemed to show up and provide in the nick of time—whether it was food we needed or people to eat it.

It was the day of our big Thanksgiving feast. We had been passing out invitations, especially to our unhoused neighbors, and had done a food drive for nonperishables. We'd recruited volunteers to make turkey and stuffing, cranberry sauce, mashed potatoes, and pie. I had planned it down to every detail.

And then it poured. Our church without walls was also a church without a roof. I had prepared a sermon on practicing gratitude, and had to take my own counsel as I muttered while carrying a big tub of plates and cups through the muddy garden out the front gates and across the street: "I'm grateful for our neighbors for letting us use their space as a backup in the rain. I'm grateful I'm not the only one who is schlepping all of the things we need for worship from our shed in the garden through the mud and across the street." I put on a smile, took off my raincoat and adjusted my slightly damp clergy collar, and walked in to see a buzz of people setting up.

Bree, a friend of Nora's who was getting more and more involved, led the food drive assembly on one side of the event space. Recently laid off from her job at a downsizing nonprofit, Bree put her social work degree and experience to work as a volunteer with us. She was standing at the door when a mother in her late sixties and her adult son walked up. "Is the Garden Church meeting today?" they asked. "This is our first time." Bree put them straight to work putting granola bars and tuna packets into bags. After worship, the son kept saying, "I really needed that today. I really needed to hear that. I really needed this. This saved me." I didn't find out until a few weeks later about the depression and insomnia he was living with.

One of our youngest volunteers and her mother came through the doors. She asked as we were packing the food bags, "Can I take one of these to the man I saw in the wheelchair down the street?" Of course, we said. Bree had seen this man before church as she'd been parking. She had found an invitation to the Thanksgiving Celebration and Dinner on the welcome table and had walked back down the street to give it to him. As we were in the middle of communion, he rolled in. He pulled out his invitation and showed it to Bree, who was standing at the door welcoming people.

"I have an invitation," he said, "Can I come in?" as if he needed to prove he was welcome. My heart ached. How often is he turned away? I wondered. Bree came back to the circle and caught my eye to make sure I'd seen that he came in, and I went over to share communion with him. My young helper followed with the cup.

I knelt down and said, "Beloved child of God, the body of Christ broken for you." He crossed himself, looked upward, and opened his mouth like a baby bird—or a staunch Catholic—and I placed the bread in his mouth. "Amen." Then our young server walked up to his chair, looking in his face right at her eye level, and poured him the cup. He took it in his weathered hands.

"I was a Eucharistic minister in the Catholic church," he said later, as we were rearranging tables after worship, preparing for the feast. "I was trained to take people who couldn't get out of their homes communion. I can give communion too. So, what kind of priest are you?" he continued. "I know you're not Catholic because women can't be—are you Episcopalian?" We talked about Protestants and Catholics, priests and laity, and the many branches of the Christian family tree. He told me how he had been raised Lutheran, was a Vietnam veteran, and after the war, he and his wife had converted after finding a Catholic church they really liked. "That was years ago," he said, "Before my wife died, and before my legs stopped functioning. Before this." He pointed down at the wheelchair and then quickly changed the subject by asking about getting a plate of food.

As dinner began, more and more people came in. Some had gone out on the streets to find others, reminding them that Thanksgiving dinner was tonight with the Garden Church. The Holy Spirit did her work—people kept coming, and coming, and coming. Wet and cold and hungry people. There was an incredible abundance of rain. There was an incredible abundance of thanksgiving.

My personal struggle with an orientation of scarcity became more exposed as I wrestled with it in community. Scarcity is at the root of the belief systems that can tear us apart in community and widen class divides. The orientation of scarcity can breed insularity and the self-serving impulse to make everyone we encounter either a member of or an outcast from our particular group, in order to validate and ensure our own survival.

But what if everyone has something they are hungry for *and* everyone has something to offer? What kind of life-giving expressions of church might exist if we were oriented towards collaboration and abundance, drawing from and appreciating the specific gifts and offerings each tradition or denomination brings, while coming together to collaborate in ministry and expressions of church in our communities? What might happen in our food systems and our economic systems if we focused on collaboration and generosity, rather than the accumulation of wealth for a few at the expense of the many?

In her book *Love Big*, author and leadership consultant Rozella Haydée White writes about how a "faith in scarcity" can cause people to "hoard resources out of the fear that there is not enough for all to be sustained." She writes that "this belief in scarcity has taken root in many of us, leading us away from each other and from ourselves. Faith in scarcity is deadly, and I don't believe in anything that takes life. I only believe in that which creates life."[1]

There are many ways to do this work of reorienting our lives from scarcity towards justice and generosity, and more and more I believe it is crucial to our survival. At the Garden Church, being church together was giving us an opportunity to pay attention to each other's needs and genuinely care about each other. We were reminded that if we looked around and saw what we had, and then asked God's blessing and shared it with others, there would be enough—enough and some to share.

I preached about gratitude that Thanksgiving, but not as merely a reminder to say thank you because "it's that season."

Rather, we need revolutionary gratitude—the kind that can change how we approach the world and each other, shifting us from "I want, I need, it's all about me" to seeing how we have enough to share.

The words of our blessing song, written by my friend Kerri Meyer from St. Gregory's, speak to the call away from scarcity. "There is enough, there is enough, there is enough, enough and some to share" was Kerri's heart response to reading the works of Wendell Berry, as well as her own craving for a theology of abundance. The song weaves together words of creation, of Elijah visiting a poor widow, of loaves and fishes, the community of Acts, and the vision and longing for the kingdom of God. "The song comes out of the times when I have been without an income, relying on my wife, Jen, and we've only been scraping by in a place where I swear the economy is weighted in favor of the Empire," Kerri told me. "I want to be generous, so I have to believe these words. I want to be able to receive generosity, so I have to believe these words: 'There is enough and some to share' as the opposite of what the idol of capitalism demands we believe. It's the motto of another possible world."[2]

As the Thanksgiving celebration came to a close, I invited everyone to turn to the person next to them and share what they were grateful for. I looked around the room, overflowing with food and laughter and smiles, and all different kinds of people, and saw a glimpse of this other world that is possible.

"I saw God in being able to invite my friends to come and experience my special church," said Denyse, who had arrived at some point with friends. Jarrett sauntered in with his lanky legs swinging in frayed shorts, followed by a young woman with a skateboard and pink and green hair. She sat down with him at a table with a middle-aged couple who were living in their car.

"Is it okay if my dog comes in too?" the woman asked. The kids ran over to pet it. "I see God in my pup," she said. "When she rests, I know I need to rest; when it's time to go for a walk, I go. She takes care of me."

A young woman with dark curly hair and a thick camo coat came in about halfway through the meal and got a plate. As we began asking everyone around the circle where they saw the presence of God today, she shared, "I was at the bus stop, wondering and worrying where and how I was going to eat tonight, and this guy went by on a bike and said, 'There's free food down the street,' and so I turned around and came here." She started crying as she spoke. "I'm just so grateful. I didn't know where I was going to eat, and here you all are."

Afterwards I heard more of her story. She had been living on the streets for five months. "I have come close to giving up so many times, but I have a daughter, and I keep going for her." She explained how she had lost custody of her daughter because of being unhoused, but was having a hard time getting housing because she didn't have a child in her custody. She was falling through the cracks of the system. I affirmed how hard it all is.

"Can we pray with you?" I asked.

"Yes, please," she said.

Little Leia's mom, Sarah, was walking by and I asked if she would pray too. All three of us were teary by the end. Reaching inside her thick camo coat, the young mom pulled out her phone to show us photos of her smiley-faced little girl.

"How old?" Sarah asked.

"Two and a half," she answered.

The look on Sarah's face deepened. "Same as my Leia," she said quietly. As Sarah and the mom continued to talk, I went to find food and blankets. What we could offer seemed so inadequate. I wanted to change the system and get housing for all these people and provide the medical care and jobs and care they needed . . . but somehow a plate of food, a prayer, a hug can be enough for the moment. The community still needed to change, to provide for everyone, but for tonight, there was enough to keep going.

-5-

GOD IS HERE

In the beginning was the Word, and the Word was with God and the Word was God, and God came and dwelt among us, God came and pitched her tent among us, God came and set up his tabernacle among us."

We spoke these words each week as we began our worship service together on Sunday afternoons at four o'clock. Making and being church, however, started about an hour earlier, when we'd pull out the hoses for watering and circle around the whiteboard to figure out what the garden work was for the day.

Our weekly Sunday gathering included three movements: working together, worshiping together, and eating together. We were striving to create a permeable space—come for what you are interested in, stay as long as you want. If you were not into gardening, you would not be forced to pull weeds or turn the compost. You could do some art at the picnic table, or join in practicing music for worship, or just sit and enjoy the sun.

If staying for worship sounded unappealing, you were free to keep weeding at the edges and listen from a distance—we would even bring communion to you if that were more comfortable. If you were hungry and just wanted the meal, you did not have to listen to a sermon before you ate. Everyone was welcome to everything, but also to come and go as they felt led. God was in it all.

I felt it my call as a pastor to continue pointing to and proclaiming this gospel, the good news: God is everywhere and moving in all things, and God is right here with us. As I spoke the invocation each week, we framed our time together with those words from the gospel of John. I would look out over the fluctuating group of people circled around on benches, blankets, and camping chairs, and say those well-worn words, sometimes feeling that God was with us, and other times willing it to be true.

Over the years leading up to planting the Garden Church, I reflected on the essentials of worship and church, studied various ecclesial traditions, and observed and participated in many worship services. I prayed and wondered: What are the things we really *need* to have collective worship?

Our Garden Church worship service drew on an eclectic mix: communion liturgy adapted from St. Gregory's Episcopal Church mixed with the Swedenborgian Book of Worship. Our confession and assurance came from the liturgy from Iona Abbey, an ecumenical community in the Isles of Scotland. Our songs came from the long shelf of hymnals and songbooks I had from many traditions, and some that my sister Nora wrote for us.

Before the very first gatherings of the Garden Church, when we met in parks around San Pedro, I walked around my house, finding things I guessed we would need for worship. I picked up my Bible with the canvas cover I'd been given for my ordination, a candle in a holder from a friend. A white ceramic tree of life icon that Sara had brought back from her trip to Turkey. I grabbed the stainless steel water bottle and matching stainless cups that I had ordered as Garden Church–worthy communion ware, and carefully wrapped them in shawls and scarves. I placed everything in the big woven basket I found in Ghana during my college days. In this basket went the freshly baked gluten-free bread for communion, a bottle filled with grape juice, and another with water for the little baptismal bowl.

My years of study and reflection led me to believe that we did need *some* things, some physical items, to be a church. These tangible elements, and the way we interacted with them, help form us as spiritual community over time. Our church in a basket was unpacked every time we stopped and made camp. It was our tabernacle.

Each Sunday, I would lift up a copy of the Bible and say, "The stories of God and the stories of humanity," as I opened it and placed it on the cedar stump in the center of the sanctuary. Next, I would light the candle and invoke the words from the first chapter of the gospel of John, proclaiming the light of Christ that shines in the darkness and is not overcome. I invited people to look around and remember that it is also the light they are seeing in each other's eyes—that divine spark in every human being. If children were there for worship, I would then invite them to help me pour water. As it flowed from the stainless steel bottle into the ceramic bowl that lived on our altar and doubled as a bee bath, we would remember the water of life and of baptism, the water that renews us and reminds us that each and every moment is an opportunity for a new beginning. Then I would dig in the basket, along with the children, until we found the bread and the cup for communion. I lifted them high in the air as a reminder that we were gathered around God's table where all are welcome to feed and be fed.

Finally, our tree of life icon, with its bright red fruit and vibrant green leaves in relief from the white ceramic tile, would be passed around the circle, reminding us of the picture God was calling us to embody. The city is described as a celestial urban environment with trees and the river in it. As each person held and felt the icon, we talked about this vision as calling forth a new way of being in the world, of being beloved community, of being church. We would examine the tree's twelve types of fruit: one for every month. All kinds of food for all kinds of people. Its leaves are said to be "for the healing of the nations" (Revelation 22:2). As we looked at the icon of this sacred tree, we remembered how the vision places it in the middle of the holy city. In Revelation 21:22, John writes that in this city there is no temple, because God is everywhere.

As we remembered these manifestations of God's vision, we would notice we were standing in an empty lot in downtown San Pedro. This was our little part of God's city, where we were called to cultivate those healing leaves—the peace, justice, love, and compassion in the world. Our theology was informed by the surrounding city, our liturgy was shaped by the humanity that came through our gates, and our words, hearts, actions, and prayers were molded by our immediate world. As we were transforming this plot of land into an urban farm and outdoor sanctuary, our very lives, and the life of community, were being transformed as well.

The Garden Church was a church without walls, literally in the heart of the city, permeable to all around us. The noise of helicopters blended into the sound of people's voices as they planted and weeded together, sweating in the heat. We didn't need stained glass windows and carved pews, strictly held doctrines, or specific codes of belonging to find the God of heaven and earth. As we kept showing up each week, we were awed together that God was moving in all things. Indeed, God was right there, with us.

I purposefully began weekly worship at the Garden Church by naming how we were a community *on the move*, a community that was becoming, forming, and exploring who God was calling us to be. It was on purpose that we began church by unpacking our Garden Church tabernacle.

In Hebrew, the word translated as "tabernacle" is *mishkan*—the "residence" or "dwelling place" of God. The image goes back to the ancient stories of the people of Israel wandering in the desert. They had escaped slavery in Egypt and were heading towards the Promised Land, the land flowing with milk and honey. This journey went on for forty years, and the people of Israel were not always keen about it; they would complain about their circumstance, whine about God and Moses, their leader, and even wish that they were back in slavery. But every time they stopped on their journey, they would set up the tabernacle.

At every stop they took time to painstakingly put each pole in its proper spot, place each carefully measured support, the layers of cloth, and the sacred objects. In the outer part of the tent they would place an oil lamp, a table for bread, and the altar of incense. In the inner tent, the holy of holies, was the ark of the covenant, with the two stone tablets that held the

Ten Commandments, God's words to them. There was also a golden urn holding manna. These sacred objects reminded them who they were as a community, who God was, and that God was present with them.

Just like me putting that framed photo on my dresser, or setting up our Garden Church table, they made an intentional space, over and over. Here is home for this moment. Here is God with us. Here is where we belong.

December's shifting sun meant it was dusk by the time our Sunday dinner rolled around. It grew cooler, too. We purchased and borrowed big patio heaters for people to huddle around. All through Advent, we gathered people together for worship with the song "O Come, O Come, Emmanuel." Nora walked in and out of the garden beds with her guitar, with the children singing and trailing after her, "O come, O come, Emmanuel, and ransom captive Israel . . ." Being outside in the elements brought Advent into focus for me. During worship we needed the heaters and the blankets that Karen had crocheted for us. Those of us with homes stepped back to make room for those living outdoors in the cold and damp. Nora and I stood side by side trying to warm each other as we watched our unhoused neighbors move in close. The cold in my hands did not seem so important when Betty's chapped hands were reaching out for heat as well. For just a couple of hours a week, I was given a tactile reminder of the weather conditions my neighbors were living in every day and night.

After my days at the Garden Church, I came home to my climate-controlled apartment, growing increasingly aware of the environment around me. My friend Nikki Cooley grew up in the Diné Nation, where her elders taught her an intrinsic connection with the land, air, animals, and plants. This interconnection makes her exquisitely in tune with the world around her and the ways that the climate is shifting and changing more and more swiftly. In an interview with an Arizona public radio station about the effects of climate change, Nikki shared that plants and other items that members of her tribe gather for ceremonies are not growing during the specified time for harvest. "If they can't harvest fish because they're not spawning and they're not regenerating, they can't hold their annual celebration in honor of the fish. So that throws off that calendar, and that just doesn't feel right to them, and that's very concerning. That has these ripple effects of the mental and spiritual impacts, not just the physical impacts that they're seeing."[1]

Nikki's deep attentiveness teaches me.

As I paid more attention to the natural world, to the people and plants and rain and drought, I was humbled and agitated by what I was learning and seeing. The negative impacts of environmental degradation and climate change often take the greatest toll on the poor, on those already struggling with asthma from air pollution, hunger due to crop failure related to climate change, and the devastation wrought by hurricanes and tropical storms, among many other challenges. The reality of the incarnated, eternal God walking in human form on earth became less abstract for me as I pastored the flow of people who came and went through our gates—the homeless, the young and pregnant, the immigrant, the wanderer, the prophets in torn clothing with shaggy hair. The stories of Christ's time on earth were often in my mind as I watched our transient neighbors bundle up after Sunday service and return to the streets. I noted the young woman at the picnic table with a five-month-old son whose stroller doubled as storage for their clothing and shared bedding as they made their way from the shelter to someone's couch to the shelter again. I thought of Mary and Joseph, far from home, looking for a place not only to sleep but for Mary to give birth, and finding only closed doors.

Throughout December, the dirt hard beneath my boots and the chilly wind catching my words as I said the invocation, the apostle John's poetic rendering of the incarnation of Christ took on flesh.

> In the beginning there was the Word;
>   the Word was in God's presence,
>   and the Word was God.
> The Word was present to God from the beginning.
> In the Word was life,
>   and that life was humanity's light—
>   a Light that shines in the darkness,
> A Light that the darkness has never overtaken.
> (John 1:1-2, 4-5 TIB)[2]

It was the "in-flesh" idea that kept returning to me. The great loving God of the universe understands that gritty, dry feeling when your hands have been in the dirt and you don't have access to warm water and gentle soap. The God of the universe understands that sensation in the pit of the stomach when it has been too long since you have had food, and the parched feeling of not enough to drink. The God of the universe sees those who have traveled far from home, escaping harm and seeking safety and care for their families. Divinity came and in-fleshed itself here among us, among our neighbors as they were quite literally pitching their tents, huddled down by the post office and in the park by the bridge. Born through a woman far from home and away from all she knew, in a shed, behind the inn, with the animals, and visited by shepherds, God Incarnate had pitched a tent among us.

As we prepared for our first Christmas Eve in the garden, I was reminded again of the things one takes for granted in an established church. I searched for and found the right-sized baby doll—one with brown skin like Jesus—and then began looking around for branches to build a manger for him. The groundskeeper at Wayfarers Chapel had just the thing. He kindly cut branches from the big thick bush he had just trimmed in two- and four-foot lengths for me. I pulled my car out of my garage, which doubled as the "church basement," and turned the concrete floor into a workshop. As I nailed the two sets of branches into crosses and then wired a bed of smaller branches onto the structure, I thought about the original manger: what kind of wood was it made of, and how had they fastened the pieces together?

On Christmas Eve, the manger went in the back of my car, along with a big tub of Christmas lights, thermoses of hot water and tea and cocoa, and the baby Jesus doll, cradled in a pile of lap blankets.

In the garden, a young artist in the area who had been leading meditative art exercises during our Work Together times spread out the Christmas tree ornaments made over the last few weeks. Everyone would be receiving one as a gift that evening. Jedidiah, who preferred to be called Jedi, reached up his lanky teenage arms, and Nora deftly climbed the ladder as they strung Christmas lights and connected them to the newly installed, solar-powered battery while chatting about family Christmas traditions. Jedi was a sophomore in high school when he began volunteering and attending the Garden Church. His mom wanted him to have a space that "was his," and she faithfully dropped him off at Work Together time and then picked him up after dinner. A self-avowed agnostic, Jedi fluctuated between asking involved, insightful questions and sitting on the edge of the circle or continuing to work in the Garden when it came time for worship.

Jedi was always willing to jump in and help. This Christmas Eve was no exception. Jedi said his sister liked to string lights, and Nora spoke of our childhood tradition of Christmas carols and candles at bedtime. I placed the manger and began weaving stalks of lavender, bunches of rosemary, and even a bit of Swiss chard and basil between the branches to create a soft, fragrant bed for baby Jesus. I nestled in the doll, wrapped tightly in cream-colored muslin, and placed a few zinnias, marigolds, and calendula flowers around his head, creating a glowing halo around the Christ Child.

A few hours later I stood beside the manger and looked the precious community in the eyes. I handed each of them a candle and they leaned over to adore the Christ. "Baby!" exclaimed Leia, in that way that only toddlers who feel grown up can do. She bent over the manger and buried her face in the flowers and herbs as she planted a wet kiss on the doll's face. The smell of basil wafted toward me as her glowing face looked up at me. "Me kiss baby Jesus!" she proudly proclaimed.

One of the ideas that I carry forward from my Sweden-borgian heritage is the concept that the entire natural world is infused with spiritual reality, and that the Divine is always pressing and urging to be received. That the Divine came to earth, to this natural world, in the body of Jesus Christ, *and* that the Divine is infused in all things of this natural, bodily world. Emmanuel, God with us, is here with us.

While we at the Garden Church saw this in the specifics of our space and lives, it also reminded us that this in-breaking goes so much farther—it goes out to the broken bodies, the battered hearts, and the abused land. Love is constantly push-ing, urging, renewing, and healing. The promise of incarnation is this pattern: God shows up in the midst of all, loving all. This love is born inside each of us and calls us, in turn, to love. The Love, the Light, is always breaking in, and it is our job to pay attention to that love in the world.

We paid attention to it in the people who came through our gates, in the community around the table, and in the actual garden itself, as plants reached their roots down while leaves and flowers reached for the sun. As we tended to carrots and beets, as we watered and picked the seemingly endless harvest of Swiss chard, we found connection with the Divine. As one of my favorite writers and theologians, Madeleine L'Engle, wrote, "There is nothing so secular that it cannot be sacred, and that is one of the deepest messages of the Incarnation."[3]

We created a ritual for our closing circle each week at the end of the gathering. After dinner, people would put their food scraps in the compost and give their paper plates to Randy, who meticulously ripped them up to prepare them for the compost. We would gather back around the altar in the mid-dle of the sanctuary space for our closing circle. After getting everyone's attention, I would say, "Here at the Garden Church we believe that God is everywhere and moving in all things *and* that God is right here with us . . . and so we end our gatherings with a ritual we call 'Where did you see God today?' Where did you touch, taste, hear, see, feel the presence of the divine? And after each person shares, we'll sing the refrain together: God is here."

People would look around for a minute and think, and then someone might say:

"I saw God when I woke up this morning and saw the sunrise and knew it was a new day."

God is here, we'd all sing.

"I tasted God today in that amazing lasagna Fred baked."

God is here.

"I saw God today when I was about to yell and hit a friend in an argument, but instead I stopped, and we were able to reconcile."

God is here.

Little Leia would jump up and down and sing "God is here" each time and then eagerly say, "Again, again!"

"I saw God in the tomatoes that we planted this summer and harvested and ate today."

God is here.

"I saw God around this circle in each of these faces coming together and being church together."

God is here.

"When I was planting basil with Jimmy and found out that we shared a hometown in common."

God is here.

We engaged this spiritual practice of noticing God's presence in our midst to see more clearly the power of the incarnation.

I noticed God working in the interactions between people, in the wind blowing through the lemon tree, in the little bursts of energy when I was exhausted, and in the way people kept showing up to feed and be fed together. *God was there. God is here.*

In her book *Grounded*, author and scholar Diana Butler Bass talks in depth about how she sees our culture engaging with a God who leaves the building and is found in the natural world. She reflects that this has always been true—we are just seeing it in different ways in this generation.[4] It felt as though the Garden Church was taking up that challenge by looking at how a spiritual community could engage directly with the natural world around us. We were experiencing that church could be a place to gather in the middle of things, rather than a space set apart in quiet seclusion. As we named incarnation, claiming and remembering God's presence everywhere, church itself became part of the interconnection of all things. As we sang, prayed, wept, and laughed together, as we felt the earth beneath our feet and God's breath in the wind, I heard people's voices talking to me and talking to each other, and the conversation went something like this . . .

"I feel God in the earth . . ."

"We see God in each other . . ."

"Well, if *this* is church . . ."

"I belong . . ."

These voices joined with the conversation that was and is building, being murmured between church leaders and sociologists, written about by statisticians and prophetic voices, sung out on the streets. This is the growing headline: *God is on the move*. Or maybe: *People are on the move*. Or both. Whatever it is, we are not looking for God in the predictable ways and places as much anymore, or connecting with God through "proper" hierarchical channels. It seems that this God who has always been everywhere and moving in all things is moving directly with us.

Certainly, there was a time, not so long ago, in the general mainstream Christian movements, when we thought we knew where God was. God was that great and powerful force, distant, up in heaven, proclaiming things. This was the God whom people would ask why bad things happened, the one to be careful not to upset or disappoint. God was also in the churches and places of worship. Where special buildings and special people and special language could invoke him—and yes, it was almost always a *him*—and there were particular procedures and formulas for connecting with God. Hymns were written, prayers prayed, theology penned, narratives woven, and generations formed around those narratives. And if you were the church type, a religious type, this is where you found God, in the church and in the heavens.

But that is not the whole story. Heretics and faithful people throughout the generations have looked for God in the rocky shores of the Scottish coastline and the scorching sand of Egypt's desert, in the basements of community centers, and on the streets praying and singing in protest. As the religious and spiritual landscapes of the world are changing, people are becoming less and less dependent on traditional forms of church for their connection to God and community.

Church attendance has been on a steady decline for years in the United States, across denominations, and people are changing how they identify themselves in the world. No longer are "Methodist" or "Lutheran," let alone "Quaker" or "Swedenborgian," common responses when asked about religious affiliation. Even "Christian" seems to be going out of style. The fastest growing groups are those who check "none" when asked about religion, or who identify as "spiritual but not religious."[5] The way we relate to God and each other, and to spirituality and community, continues to change. Maybe the work of the religious is not to be gatekeepers and jury, making sure that only the approved and specifically righteous, those with correct beliefs and right behavior, encounter the holy. Instead, maybe our job is to pay attention to how God is moving in the world, to God with us, and to how all creation is holy. Maybe our task is to be the heralds and cultivators of our time.

My hunger for a collective recognition of the holy herewith-us has not been held alone. While I appreciate the freedom to find God at brunch with friends, or alone near the mountain stream, I also crave worshiping in community, and hallowing that which is with us.

And whether we were nonreligious, spiritual-but-notreligious, disenfranchised, or deeply devout, we at the Garden Church were people hungry for collective hallowing, noticing the holy as we pulled the candle, the bread, the cup, out of the basket, as we knelt and dug the potatoes out of the soil, as we sat and ate the harvest together.

I kept hearing from people that they longed for places where there was freedom to take down walls and release the need to be gatekeepers of the correct way of seeing God. People were searching for religious leaders whose focus wasn't on trying to convert people to a specific set of beliefs, and instead were invested in trusting God's ever-present work of transformation. People were hungry for a place to belong, to be loved, to be seen just as they are, in the uniqueness and variety of the human family. People were hungry to connect with the earth, with each other, with God. I knew I was hungry for it.

The call to pay attention is one God has been speaking to God's people throughout the generations. I'm reminded of the children of Israel receiving this lesson after their exodus from Egypt. As Exodus 16 recounts, the children of Israel, wandering in the desert and toting their tabernacle with them, were exhausted and hungry. God heard them and said there would be bread from heaven. They woke up one morning and saw that "when the layer of dew lifted, there on the surface of the wilderness was a fine flaky substance, as fine as frost on the ground" (Exodus 16:14).

But they did not say, "Oh, look, God provided for us!" No, instead they said, "Manna?" which means, "What is it?" And then they named it *manna* and they did not eat it but instead continued to go hungry.

So Moses pointed it out to them and said something like, "People, *this* is the bread that the Lord has given you to eat."

They finally realized. They bent down, scooped it up, and took it to their tents to prepare and eat.

This is as true for us today as it was for our ancestors centuries ago. What we need is all around us: in the gifts of community and in God's provision, which comes in unexpected ways. At the Garden Church, as we kept coming together around that table, we found that there was enough healing, reconciliation, hope, connection, and food for everyone. And when it was easy to overlook, to miss what was there, we learned to be Moses for each other. We came together and reminded each other how God calls us to stop, look, and ask, "What is it?" and then bend down and pick up that heavenly goodness, that which sustains.

In our little plot in the middle of the city, we gathered around God's table, where all are welcome, where all you had to be to eat was hungry, with the sky above our heads and the earth beneath our feet, in the middle of the city, and proclaimed, "God is here!"

I have often said, then and since, that the Garden Church was the closest to the kingdom of God I'd ever experienced. And while true, it is also true that in the end it was not uniquely qualified to receive God's presence with us. I saw it in the people there because it was my job as their pastor to pay attention, to look for it and see it in them as we recognized and celebrated the places that Emmanuel God was showing up.

In the Orthodox Church, one of the jobs of the deacon is this: before the reading of Scripture, the deacon stands tall and at attention, and in a strong voice calls out, "Wisdom, attend!" Is this not the job of the faithful? To pay attention, to be present, to notice and point to the presence of God with us? The provision is there, the dew is stretched over the ground. It is up to us to look around and ask, "What is it?" and to bend down and pick up this bread from heaven.

Look at the vegetable stand with basil and rosemary.

Look at that toddler's dimpled grin.

Look at the rich purple hue of that eggplant!

Look at how that man whom we see walking by on his way to and from the bar becomes our friend.

Look at the rich earth.

Look at God with us!

-6-

THE WATER OF LIFE

Leia, I baptize you in the name of the Father, the Son, and the Holy Spirit, our Creator, Sustainer, and Redeemer, the One who is, and who was, and who is to come." As my hand dripped water, I caressed the toddler's forehead. She smiled and squirmed in her mother's arms. Her mother's face was filled with a deep smile. Her father stood behind with tears in his eyes.

It was perhaps this first baptism at the Garden Church that solidified us as a church. Leia's parents had approached me at the end of the community meal one winter evening. "We never thought we'd find a church we'd want our child to be part of, but this is it," they said. I had done baptisms before, and the sacrament in itself is always a powerful reminder of belonging to God and belonging to each other. But a family was choosing this specific community, the church we had started, and committing their child to God and to our particular collection of the saints.

Sarah had grown up in Catholic school, and Ed had religious experiences and was deeply read in religious texts, but had little interest in organized religion. This family said they didn't fit in a traditional church, and yet they wished for a spiritual community for Leia, their first child, but had found nothing comfortable for them. Until they found us.

The first summer we were open, Sarah and Leia had come through the gates on a Friday morning. Leia wandered from the table to the watering cans to the garden beds, and back again. Sarah found solace in the liturgy, inclusive theology, and preaching. After a few weeks, Ed started showing up around dinnertime. A few weeks later, he started coming earlier. One day he took communion when I offered it to him. Soon Sarah's parents, Peter and Linda, began to attend too, and Ed and Peter dove into our project of building a new shed with solar panels on the roof. Meanwhile, Sarah spearheaded our parents and tots group—Little Sprouts—helping to nurture the community she wanted to raise her daughter in.

I saw all this happening, but was still delighted and surprised when they approached me with the question: "Would you baptize Leia, here at the Garden Church?"

Leading up to the baptism day, we talked through it all: what baptism meant—and didn't mean—to them and how the service would go. As we gathered together in our sanctuary that day, I preached on baptism; that this baptism was for Leia and her parents and family, but this was also a baptism for our church. As we baptize into the broader church, the communion of saints, we also baptize into the specific church, the people who surround each one of us on our journey of faith.

In the Swedenborgian tradition, we baptize as infants, or anyone at any age they desire to be baptized. Some traditions wait until a person is a bit older and able to make the choice for themselves. Some baptize via full immersion into the water, others by making the sign of the cross in water on the forehead, others by pouring water over the head. The various means of baptism across the Christian tradition are traced back to John the Baptizer, who baptized Jesus on the banks of the Jordan River. The gospel of Luke reads that after Jesus was baptized, "heaven was opened, and the Holy Spirit descended upon him in bodily form like a dove. And a voice came from heaven, 'You are my Son, the Beloved; with you I am well pleased.'" (Luke 3:21-22). I picture the blessing that Jesus received as being the blessing for us all—regardless of specific baptismal tradition.

All sorts of people came together to create our church's baptism. The white tablecloths came out. Flowers were bought and arranged. A huge feast appeared. Extra hands pitched in. Connie, simultaneously a devout Catholic and a Garden Church member, put together a beautiful art project in honor of Leia: writing blessings and wishes on tissue paper and then wrapping them around a candle. Connie also asked her eighty-three-year-old Italian mother to make a cake—"She made cakes for all of my children's sacraments when they were young," she told me. Stephanie showed up with a beautiful basket filled with gifts for Leia "from the church," including a little plastic green dinosaur so she could take home her very own Dino. My sister Nora worked with Leia's father, Ed, and her grandparents, Peter and Linda, to put together special music for the service. Their guitar, mandolin, and voices blended into a group that turned out to be repeat players at many future services.

After Leia was baptized and blessings were given, I invited everyone to circle around and lay on their hands. "God loves you and a whole lot of people love you, Leia," said one woman as she reached out her hands to bless the toddler.

As we circled back around the table for communion, the feeling of community was palpable. There were over fifty people there. Our sanctuary felt full and vibrant. During dinner, my friend and colleague Rev. Jonathan, who was visiting from San Diego for the service, said, "Looks like a church. Acts like a church. I think it's a church."

"I think it's a church," I repeated.

But being a church seemed to have as many hard, hopeless moments as it did big, beautiful ones. As we walked through late winter and Lent, I found my inner reserves waning. I wondered how long I could keep up the energy and pace required to start a church, a farm, and a nonprofit—and fund it, pastor it, lead it, and hold hope.

My week revolved around Sunday but included much more than preparation for our weekly gathering. Starting a new church, as well as a farm, brought a learning curve for each new necessity—budgets and fundraising, garden design and soil structure. I met with people in the community regularly, providing pastoral care to parishioners, networking with local business owners and nonprofit leaders, and working with local clergy. I found myself working longer and longer hours; there was always more to do to keep things running at the garden. And I was feeling more and more deeply the systemic injustices at work in the lives of the people in the community of San Pedro.

The water of life came to me in the form of people, like Connie and Peter and Linda and Nora's friend Bree, who kept showing up over the course of that winter. And in the form of a really big leap of faith from the board, which agreed to hire Bree—if I could raise the money for her salary.

Bree had become increasingly involved over the previous months. From the day she had first walked through the gates, she had felt an affinity to the work we were doing and the life and activity she saw there. "It's warm and inviting," she mused as we were weeding together one afternoon. "It's a place I would want to go into even if that hadn't been my intended destination." Rather than being scared away by a start-up, she was drawn to the fact that the Garden Church was unconventional, from the place we gathered to the people who made up the community. We were young and small, but full of possibilities, and she wanted to be part of nurturing it. Her background in social work and nonprofit programming and volunteer management, coupled with the fact that the Garden Church embodied so much of what she had always believed church should be, felt like just the right fit. We cobbled together enough funding to hire her, with the understanding that a big portion of her job would be fundraising and grant writing, along with helping me manage volunteers, events, and community outreach. It was truly water in a parched land to have another person dedicate their attention to the church.

"I can see the weight lifting from your shoulders," Bree said as we sat at Jana's kitchen table signing contracts. I could feel it too. Many volunteers supported the Garden Church. But two years of being solo in full focus had taken a toll on me.

The renewing water of baptism washed over us as we kept showing up to be a community together. The reality of the need for actual water and the struggles of drought were present. Being out in the elements connected us to the environment and the earth itself. We saw the daily realities of climate change as we carefully watered the vegetables during one of the worst droughts in California's recorded history. When I saw water being used to green people's lawns, rather than grow food or sustain other life, I winced. I found myself both frustrated and saddened. I now knew how much water it took to carefully grow this little bit of food without the help of the rain. I now knew the amount of food—and water—needed to feed the country from valleys and fields of California. When the Garden Church had to shut down for a few days because of the smoke from grass and forest fires miles away, we were reminded that our individual and collective choices were integral to the health of the overall interconnected web of life.

As I poured the water of baptism, and traced the sign of the cross, I noted that the ritual held in it both the renewing presence of God's love and the reality of the cross. In the ancient ritual of baptism, we are named and claimed by the loving God who created us, who forgives us and loves us as we are. We are baptized in the name of the Father, the Son, and the Holy Spirit, in the fullness and wholeness of God, and then in many traditions, including mine, the sign of the cross is traced on the forehead. This last gesture always strikes me as paradoxical.

The sign of the cross is a sign of struggle and temptation. It is a sign of death. Embedded in the baptismal act of being named and claimed by the God of life and renewal, we are reminded that the way of life includes death. While remembering that

God is always with us, we acknowledge the dark night of the soul, the parts of life that bring us to our knees. We acknowledge suffering and pain, injustice and brutality in the world. We remember the things that separate us from God and each other as we hold this paradox of the spiritual life and of baptism. And then, we are called to be changed, we receive God's abundant forgiveness, and we allow ourselves to be washed clean. We remember that we are all connected and all one. Baptism reminds us that we are each beloved individuals *and* part of a bigger whole—God's church on earth and the creation and humanity all together.

The words in the liturgy echoed back to me: "God, who is gracious and merciful and slow to anger and abounding in steadfast love, loves you as you are." God loves us. God forgives us, all of us. The person addicted to crack cocaine who doesn't have housing and is struggling on the street; the suburban mom who is afraid the town where she grew up doesn't feel safe for her children and wants all those living outdoors removed from her neighborhood. God is there loving us and pouring that water of life over us. And this water of life calls us both to change and to heal wounds; to bring justice to the oppressed in the same moment that it is drawing us closer to God and to each other as the water drips from our foreheads.

The first time Leia came into the Garden Church, she was drawn to the water—the big trough of water where anyone who wanted could dip a watering can and water the garden. "Agua, agua," she called as she toddled over to it. Sarah chased after her to prevent the trough from being turned into a swimming pond. Leia, like hundreds of others, was offered a watering can and shown the thirsty plants that needed a drink. It turns out watering is fun, and engaging. I have seen parents have to pry the elephant watering can out of their children's hands when it was time to go, promising, "We can come back and water again soon."

It's not just the children who like to water. It's a necessary and easy way to get anyone involved. At the Garden Church, we sought the image of God in everyone who walked through the gates. As we strove to live into our motto, "Feed and be fed," we embraced the idea that everyone has something they are hungry for *and* has something to provide. "What do you need?" we would ask. "What do you have to offer?"

We quickly found that the question of what people had to *offer* was often the more engaging one. People wanted to get involved, to experience the joy of working in the garden and nurturing the plants and the community; people wanted to give. Some who came through the gates had gardening backgrounds and could be quickly put to work planting, harvesting, or pruning. But most people didn't know much about working the land; while they wanted to learn, watering was a good place to start. "Water the roots, not the leaves," said Nancy, or whoever was welcoming at the gate. That was the extent of the training needed.

"I'm not much of a gardener," Nancy said, "but as a sailor and a seafarer"—Nancy had spent years as a sailor—"helping people to water is one of my favorite things here. And I mostly can't mess it up."

The first time Jarrett came in, he sauntered through the gates as if he owned the block. In some ways he did, having lived on these streets and alleys for many years.

"Welcome to the Garden Church!" I said in a chipper voice.

"What is this place?" he asked.

"It's a church and a garden," I replied.

"Huh. Can I garden?"

"Sure thing," I replied, "Will you help us water?"

I showed which garden beds were thirsty. He got to work. After filling the can from the water trough a few times, he got bored and asked if he could use the hose. Farmer Lara tentatively gave him the large watering nozzle. He looked earnestly at the plants as he stood over them with his lanky body, careful not to tread anything with his army boots as he moved from bed to bed. He watered for ten minutes and then was done—for the day. But the next time we were open, he was back. "Can I water again?" he asked.

This became a weekly pattern. Jarrett came in and watered, and in and amongst it he began to share bits of his story with us. "See this?" he'd say, bending down to show his tattoo to Nancy, pulling his sleeve up from spiked bracelets to reveal his arm. "These are the names of all the women I'm supposed to protect and not sleep with. What's your name? See, here it is, so you're one of the women I'm supposed to protect." Nancy chuckled and let Jarrett expound.

Nancy was so short next to him, her white hair stark against his green camo outfit. She showed him the anchor tattoo on her ankle and told him about her work with sailing and tall ships. Nancy, a fixture of the San Pedro community, had been connecting people to the Garden Church since my first scouting trip. She faithfully showed up every week, always with a new idea of how to connect us with the Girl Scouts, the elementary school, the chamber of commerce, and the gallery down the street. No one was unimportant to Nancy.

Some days I'd have the patience and pastoral energy to talk to Jarrett and hear his stories. Many other days I would give him a friendly welcome and get him water, trying to avoid the lengthy stories, mixtures of life and fantasy, delusion and pain. He reminded me regularly of the struggles of living on and off the streets.

It was clear that I couldn't make it all—or even much— better for him. I couldn't fix the problems in the community, a complicated web of housing insufficiencies, lack of health-care, few job opportunities, biased incarceration system, the toxins of patriarchy, and a limited flow of resources. It felt overwhelming to fully receive the complexity of people's sto-ries and needs.

I struggled with the tension inherent in the one-on-one interactions with the community that came through our gates. I could freely proclaim and promise that God was always giving them the chance for new life—"every day, every moment is an opportunity for a new beginning," as the liturgy says. Yet the realities of systemic oppression, racism and poverty, disdain and abuse were prevalent and obvious. I wrestled with my own place in it all, knowing that I was not merely an observer in this system; examining and changing my inner and outer behavior was essential as well. I knew that the naming of each person's belovedness that was hap-pening within those gates was important, but I also knew that much work was needed in order for there to be justice, equality, and compassion in the community. The former was important but did nothing to diminish the pressing reality of the latter.

The concept of circulatory power is a way of describing the global flow of capital. The scholar-activist Romand Coles uses the even more heightened term "mega-circulatory power" to describe flows of consumption that require human and ecological devastation *in order to* succeed.[1] Seen through this lens, success requires distance from the actual human beings, the land, and the animals that are harmed through these systems of consumption and exploitation. As long as you cannot actually *see* the person you are harming, if you don't personally encounter the sea turtle that is prematurely dying from pollution in the ocean, if you don't speak to the person living on the streets who never has had the support to get sober or a foundation for thriving, you can distance yourself from responsibility to change the systems that are harmful in the first place. This moral distancing is so easy to do. Even as someone dedicated to a specific community, I struggled with it. It is hard to realize that each individual is being affected by bigger systems, systems that others—systems that *I*—benefit from.

I developed a better understanding of circulatory power thanks to John Senior, a professor at Wake Forest Divinity School, who wrote a paper reflecting on the work of the Garden Church as well as the work of my friend and colleague Heber Brown, founder of the Black Church Food Security Network in Baltimore, Maryland. Like the Black Church Food Security Network, we sought to work in our local sphere to engage faith communities in the feeding and wellness of our surrounding community.

San Pedro neighbors the Port of Los Angeles, one of the largest ports in the country. Every day huge ships come into the port laden with merchandise, primarily from China. Ship after ship, carrying hundreds and thousands of huge containers, filled with the things that we will then buy at Target, Home Depot, and the grocery store. As the flow of merchandise is unloaded onto trucks and trains to be shipped across the country, the people in the communities around these ports suffer the negative impact, environmentally and socially, while rarely benefiting from the economic gains. This is in addition, of course, to the many, many people who suffer in the making of the merchandise in the first place. Many of our congregation members at the Garden Church carried the entirety of their possessions in shopping carts and baby strollers, in stark contrast with container after container rolling by, holding all the blankets, coats, mattresses, and clean socks that they could ever need.

In his work on the circulatory model, Senior posits that while operations like the Garden Church cannot solve all of these problems and single-handedly overturn the economic system, they actually *can* have an impact on the flow of consumption and devastation because, in one tiny vein, those who are affected are receiving humanizing attention. "Small-scale, place-based community responses to the mega-circulatory power are 'polycentric,'" writes Senior, "like rooted capillaries that extend deeply into the ground of a particular place, but decentralized, a root system without a trunk. Such 'root clods,' as [Romand] Coles calls them, create and sustain relationships among persons, communities, and the natural world, diverting the flow of resources away from dominant circulations of power towards life-giving flows."[2]

We find such interplay in the water system as well. Tracing pollution upstream, one finds that plants, animals, and people are being harmed for miles downstream by a factory dumping pollutants miles upstream. By looking at where our water comes from, we see the interconnected system of which we are a part. This can inspire focus on the care and healing of our watersheds, as well as the land connected to and affected by the movements of the water.

Our friends in the watershed discipleship movement and in the Wild Church Network introduced me to the practice of discovering and mapping one's watershed in connection to baptism.[3] In many churches in the Western world, people experience baptism in the contained and sterile setting of an indoor sanctuary. We may have a baptismal font of some kind, or a special pitcher or bowl. Rarely had I put attention to the actual water used, or thought about how this water of baptism also bonds us to the interconnected web of earth-dwellers who are reliant on water to live. When we think about the water systems in our communities in terms of the bodies or streams of water with which we could baptize—rather than assuming that clean water will be available in our church pipes—it brings our attention to another part of our interconnections in the system. In some areas, the local creek, river, pond, or—as was our case—ocean, is not clean and life-giving. You would want to be careful before swimming in it, let alone immersing, or sprinkling, your babies or yourself with polluted droplets.

When we baptize within an awareness of our watershed, we find a poignant reminder of how we belong to God, to each other, and to the larger ecosystems. In this belonging, we are both connected and responsible—not only for our own survival, but also for all with whom we are connected.

Holding this bigger picture, the immediate faces in front of us kept showing up as the work we needed to do. I hoped that by opening our gates each morning and looking people in the eyes, calling them by name, and looking for the image of God in them, we were part of a cleansing and renewing process. By bringing our attention to one small piece in this bigger system, were we helping eliminate tiny chemical dumps in our watershed or filtering an artery? Were we making a difference in the broken world we longed to heal?

Bree and I sat in the shade that was starting to creep in on the back corner of the garden. "What a roller coaster it is here," Bree reflected. "It's such an honor to know the stories of our unhoused neighbors, that people trust us with these vulnerable places." She sighed and ran her fingers through her thick brown hair. "But it also leaves me feeling so drained and helpless. The struggle that our friends are going through is so hard."

I leaned back in the blue camp chair and sighed as well. It felt like a constant challenge to stay present to the beauty and the pain that we witnessed in and amongst these garden beds.

"I guess the hard situations keep showing us the depth of the struggles. Maybe being seen and loved is something," Bree mused.

People were finding that, for a few moments at least, they were viewed as beloved within the garden gates. And yet the whole world was out there, and I could not pretend it wasn't in need of renewal and change. I continued to feel the tension between focusing right here in the space in front of me and the urge to go out into the streets, the courts, and the public forums and demand the change that was needed. I tried to make time to show up at the county commissioners' office and city hall to name the places where people needed care. It felt like any one of these areas could take all of my energy and attention, and I felt wrung dry by the expanse of the work.

Yet, somehow, we kept raising that stainless steel water bottle each week, watching the water pour into the ceramic bowl, and proclaiming that the water of life was here and flowing freely. Week after week, I pulled into the dusty back parking lot, turned off the car engine, paused for a minute to breathe, and remembered the needs in the community—needs I could no longer walk past. They were now the needs of people I had come to consider loved ones. By being present in our neighborhood and making church together with those who showed up, each person we encountered brought into focus what had once been for me simply hypothetical problems. No longer.

-7-

ASHES TO DUST, DIRT TO SOIL

I walked up to a teenage kid I had noticed before on the streets. "Ashes for Ash Wednesday?" I offered.

"Yeah, okay, yeah," he said. I asked him his name.

"Daniel," I spoke as I brushed a stringy curl off his forehead, "from dust you have come, and to dust you will return." As I spoke the words from Genesis 3:19, I traced the sign of the cross on his forehead.

He locked eyes with me, showing the vulnerability and hunger of having someone say his name, see him. His eyes filled with tears. I moved my hand from his forehead to his shoulder and offered him a blessing, "May God be with you on your way."

"Thank you, thank you," he mumbled as he walked off.

For hundreds of years, Christians have been marking the beginning of Lent—the weeks leading up to Easter—with the receiving of ashes on Ash Wednesday. Traditionally placed on heads or clothing, ashes are now most often smudged on foreheads in the sign of the cross. This ancient practice invites us to remember our mortality and it certainly comes with a long-standing power. This simple ritual, taken *outside* church walls, invited connection within our community in a new and primal way.

On the first Wednesday morning of Lent, I stood under a shade tent in the Garden Church sanctuary, going over music and the order of worship for our first collaborative Ash Wednesday service. I was glad to have a colleague with me today: Pastor Lisa from the Methodist church right down the street. Lisa got what it meant to minister to the community; she too considered everyone in the community her congregation. When I had suggested offering ashes on the streets of our neighborhood, she'd said, "Yes, of course!"

Lisa had first noticed the Garden Church on a First Thursday art night soon after being appointed the pastor at the San Pedro United Methodist Church. When we met for tea a few weeks later, she told me that her first thought when she saw it was, "Wow, they had an idea that I should have had—I could do that." We had quickly become friends, and explored together what it meant to be pastors to all in this part of our town.

At noon I rang the singing bowl we used in worship, and a few of us at the center of the garden raised our voices together in song as a signal for others to gather. When a group had congregated, we rose. Lisa's voice rang out across the din of the traffic:

Have mercy on me, O God.
Create in me a clean heart, O God,
And put a new and right spirit within me. (Psalm 51:1, 10)

As her voice rose over the cars going past and the helicopter overhead, I looked around at the faces in the circle. Alongside Garden Church regulars were people from the Methodist and Presbyterian churches, as well as those who had seen a flyer or received an invitation: the grandma with her two-year-old grandson, the owner of the gallery down the street on her lunch break, and the janitor from the Methodist church. I loved the collaboration and the spirit of openness and freedom we felt taking this ancient ritual outdoors, surrounded by soil and grit.

After we read Scriptures, I raised my hands over the ash and proclaimed: "'From dust you have come, and to dust you will return.' Almighty God, you have created us out of the dust of the earth: Grant that these ashes may be to us a sign of our mortality and penitence, that we may remember that it is by your gracious gift that we are given everlasting life. Amen."

People came forward one by one, brushing the hair away from their foreheads to expose their bare skin to this connection with mortality. Lisa's red hair framed her face as she smiled and looked into the eyes of one of the neighbors who often slept on her church steps. After prayer and another song, we invited people to come out into the community with us. Most stayed or went back about their work in the garden, or returned to their offices, but a few were ready and joined us in taking the ashes out into the streets.

I felt a tightness in my chest as we walked towards the gates. It was one thing to proclaim boldly the words and sacrament inside our own sanctuary; it felt a bit frightening to do so on the street. You'd think I'd be used to it by now—having a church outdoors in an empty lot turned urban farm, where people stuck their heads in during worship and wondered aloud what was going on.

But my insides quaked as I readied myself to make that first step beyond the garden gate. I'd read about this, I'd heard about others doing it, but I'd never actually taken ashes to the streets before. What if people said no? What if it was embarrassing? What was I leading my congregation into? I calmed myself with the knowledge that in this heavily Catholic neighborhood, at least some people would know what these ash smudges were for.

I didn't get a step beyond our front gate when someone came asking for ashes. It was Gabe, from the barbershop next door. "Do you have ashes even though I missed the service? Can I have some?"

"Of course!" I answered and reached out my hand.

"Thank you so much, I was worried I wouldn't get off work to get to church on time." We started walking up the street and popped our heads into shops along the way. We offered ashes to the people on the sidewalk as we passed. My fears were quickly allayed. The people we encountered received the ashes gratefully.

Halfway up the block we met a couple of men in their twenties in torn jeans and unbuttoned shirts. "Ashes for Ash Wednesday?" I asked.

"Uh, no thanks," one said. We all kept walking.

But the other man turned around and gave me a longing look. I raised my thumb in silent offering. He turned back towards me, lifted his shaggy bangs, and looked down shyly at the sidewalk.

"From dust you have come and to dust you will return," I said quietly as I pressed my ash-covered thumb into his forehead in the shape of a cross.

"Thanks a lot," he mumbled as he turned to join his friend.

Next we saw three older men in their lawn chairs, on the corner near the crosswalk. "Ashes for Ash Wednesday?"

"Nope, we've already been to Mass," was the answer. This was the most connection I'd ever gotten from them.

"Blessings to you!" we chorused as we walked on.

"Let's go to the shops in the walkway." Connie knew every business on the block. "I know Mary will want some," she added. We started with the jewelry shop. Indeed, the owner was glad to see Connie.

"I didn't think I was going to be able to make it to Mass today," she said. "This is so perfect."

Next the customer at the hairdresser, halfway through her appointment, jumped up and said, "Oh really? We were just talking about Ash Wednesday, thank you so much!" Her eyes filled with tears as I held up the foils on her bangs and crossed her forehead with ash.

Then the hairdresser's neighbors came over. "I was worried I wasn't going to get off work in time to get ashes," one of them said. "Thank you for bringing them to me."

As we made our way through the streets, I felt my love for this quirky town grow with each encounter. Even the people who did not want ashes appreciated the gesture. The kid at the bus stop: "I don't want the ashes to make my skin break out, but can you give me a blessing anyway?"

Each time I pressed the slightly oily ash onto someone's forehead, I felt—even if just for that moment—a dissolving of the things that separated us from each other. I generally considered myself relatively open to the people I met, but this practice stretched me to places I didn't usually tread. It was the people washing dishes in the back of the hole-in-the-wall taco joint who wanted the ashes, not the people sitting at the tables where I usually sat. The guys having a smoke out behind the mechanic's garage wanted them too. Honoring each person— whoever they were and whatever they were doing—opened up a world of connection.

I found out later that Connie, a beloved teacher of English as a second language, had continued to share the ashes that evening. As she was teaching, a student asked her about the ash cross on her forehead. "It's for Ash Wednesday," she replied, and when half her class gave her confused looks, she shared about this holiday while teaching vocabulary words.

A couple of students approached her after class. "We know Ash Wednesday, but we weren't able to get to Mass today because we had to work and then go straight to class." Connie's face fell, wishing she'd brought a container of ashes with her.

"Wait, I have an idea!" she said as she reached up to her own forehead, removing some of the ash to make the sign of the cross on her students' foreheads. "Del polvo viniste . . . y al polvo regresarás," she said softly in Spanish. "From dust you have come and to dust you will return again."

Writer and monk Thomas Merton tells a well-known story about the moment he stood on a street corner and felt unbelievable love for humanity. He writes, "In Louisville, at the corner of Fourth and Walnut, in the center of the shopping district, I was suddenly overwhelmed with the realization that I loved all these people, that they were mine and I theirs, that we could not be alien to one another even though we were total strangers. It was like waking from a dream of separateness, of spurious self-isolation in a special world."[1]

With each person whose face I looked into and touched, I felt a Merton moment—overwhelmed by a love for each person that went beyond what I could produce on my own, overwhelmed by knowing that we were all in it together. The ash on my hand and their forehead burned through my illusion that we are anything other than all in this together, mortal and human, created and beloved, dust, dirt, heart, and spirit.

We walked next to a diner where a woman joyfully bounded around the counter, "Yes, please! I want ashes! Thank you for bringing them to me!"

She turned and called to her coworkers, "Ashes!" and an old man, a young boy, the dishwasher, and the cook streamed out from the kitchen.

As we walked out, we saw an old woman in the parking lot with her life belongings loaded on a shopping cart looking up and asking for this blessing on her rugged forehead.

It is amazing to me that the desire to connect, to be seen, to be blessed, is so strong that having black ash smudged on your forehead seems like a good idea. Why would a reminder of the inevitability of death be welcomed and embraced? Perhaps it is because the ritual of the ashes brings so many dichotomies together: life and death, despair and hope, human and divine, all woven together in this sacred tactile act. Ash Wednesday is the connecting thread that takes us from the hopeful waiting of Advent to the new birth of Christmas, walks us through Epiphany and into the depths of Lent, then goes with us all the way to the death on the cross, and finally, to the new life of resurrection.

This pattern of life and death, decay and resurrection is one that chases us around, even beyond Ash Wednesday. I sometimes find myself fighting it. I want to sweep the clutter and things that are dying under the rug and focus my attention on the "hopeful new life" work. Founding a new church that claims to be reimagining church has proven to be a lightning rod for separating the old and the new into stark dichotomy. It is easy to look at all that is wrong with the church, the physically crumbling buildings, the hypocrisy in the communities, and the growing secularity in society as a whole. How easy it was for me to go down the trail of "Well, I'm planting a *new* church and we're doing it differently, and not only are we not going to have any of those problems, we also don't need any of that stuff from the past." To which I immediately hear a soft chuckle from God and my ancestors as I am reminded that what we are creating grows out of the liturgy, the wisdom, the resources, and the stories of thousands of years of people gathering together to love God and love neighbor.

Working in the garden each week supplied me with plenty of metaphors—new life from tiny seeds, pulling weeds to give space for growth, celebrating the harvest. But it was the compost heap that continued to be a guiding metaphor to me for this era of church. I wrestle with old ways of being church that need to crumble and be let go of, wondering what we can gratefully repurpose for today and what needs to be composted to become the fertile soil for something new to grow. Because, though it gives my ego a boost to believe I'm leading the "best new idea" of how to be church, I know that what I'm called to do is simply what my grandparents and great-grandparents were called to as well: to discover what it means to be faithful in our generation, for this season, in this garden. That is all we are doing: discovering the needs, gifts, questions, and doubts of this generation, and striving to create a place for people to come together. We cannot be separate from what has been. Instead, we are embedded in the rhythms and the seasons that have emerged from the past, all the while discovering what God is growing here and now as we live into that Ash Wednesday cycle. It is no mistake that ash and the dust that we come from and will return to are so connected. The compost pile shows us this: each time we examine it, we find the slimy food scraps we tossed in are being reborn into lush, rich, healthy soil. The seemingly unwanted will soon feed new life.

God takes that which is dead and dying and brings it back anew, be it a church, a life, a garden, or a community. It is this hope, this knowledge of interconnectivity, that we are reaching for when we reach for these ashes. We are reaching to know we are part of something and we matter, we are part of a bigger cycle. I like to think of it as a divine composting program.

During the first month of the Garden Church, when we were making church in public parks and on the downtown street corner, listening to our neighbors and walking our neighborhoods, we also started composting. Before we had a plot of land that we could transform, we asked ourselves what we did have—what were the resources that were already there? And how could we use them to nurture this dream? We found we had food scraps, a generous urban farmer, Lara, with a big compost bin, and people who wanted to do something to prepare the soil—literally—for the Garden Church to grow.

"Everyone in the neighborhood could be composting!" said Lara, as she and her husband, Scott, and I sat around their kitchen table after dinner. "It reduces waste, cleans the air, and makes the best soil you can get."

Scott and I nodded, the wheels in our brains churning. It could be dangerous when the two of us got going on a brainstorm.

"What about a fleet of tricycles with trailers behind them, that go around the neighborhood each week collecting full compost buckets?" Scott said.

"Yes!" I exclaimed. "Like that program we were reading about. They could also go to restaurants and schools and collect the compostables there. And maybe the hospital and hotel event center as well."

Lara brought us down to earth. "I think we need to start smaller than that."

"Right," I replied, staring off into space. We had a slowly growing group of people who were forming as the Garden Church. And they were committed to regular gatherings and being involved.

"What if wherever the Garden Church is meeting becomes a drop-off center for compostables, and we can collaborate with you at Green Girl Farms by being the guinea pigs for your composting program?" I said slowly.

"Making soil for the future garden!" Lara exclaimed.

We shared the vision with our fledgling group, including how food waste compacted in landfills is a significant contributor to greenhouse gases.[2] Although it was a gamble to engage people in collecting what is commonly thought of as garbage, people were interested. Together we learned how amazing compost is: it takes all sorts of things that are leftover, done, used, and dying—food scraps, peels, dried leaves, stale bread, even your shredded newspaper—and turns them into rich soil. It doesn't have to be fancy, it just needs to be purposeful. You put it all in a bin and let nature do its thing.

Immediately, the microscopic bacteria get to work breaking down the banana peels and the crunchy maple leaves. Then, just weeks later, a well-tended compost heap reveals its magic. Where a heap of old food scraps once was, you now find dark, rich, delightfully warm and moist soil. What just a few weeks ago made you plug your nose and run the other way now calls you to bury your face in it.

And it isn't just any old dirt. Soil from compost is rich and powerful. It improves the soil structure in which it is mixed, increases nutrient content, holds water more effectively, and wards off plant diseases, not to mention the incredible environmental impact composting makes.

The more I learned about compost, the more I saw the image of God in it, proclaiming the work she does in the world. God is the Divine Composter. She takes all that has been, all that we've used, our best bits and our slimy bits, the endings in our lives and the pain of loss, the tantalizing crumbs from our joyful moments and the leftovers we've kept for too long. God takes *all* of that and says, "Okay, great, let's see what we can do with it next!"

I often feel caught in the cross-currents between what the church has been, the parts that are dying and changing, and the church that *might* be, that which is being born. Is the job of ministry in this generation to be a hospice chaplain or a midwife? Am I caring for what is dying, or called to welcome in what is to come? I often place the state of the church in a dichotomy: what has been *versus* what is to come; old *versus* new. I either feel discouraged and paralyzed by what I cannot change, or I feel self-righteous and sure about how *I* think church should be and how it would be superior to other forms of church.

Yet the Divine Composter keeps calling me to surrender all of this to the God of resurrection, the God who doesn't waste anything, the God who takes these tensions within transition, and sees it all in the light of the cycle of life, death, and resurrection.

An image from a story in 2 Kings 2 has been following me around, a story of transition between generational leadership. Elijah, a prophet in ancient Israel, was nearing the end of his time on earth and knew that he was about to have a dramatic exit by being swept up and taken away by a whirlwind. He tried to shake loose from the young companion he had been mentoring—Elisha. Elisha kept clinging to him. Despite Elijah's efforts to remove himself, Elisha would have none of it.

"As the Lord lives, and as you yourself live, I will not leave you," the mentee proclaimed to his mentor. They continued to travel, away from Gilgal, across the Jordan River, which parted upon Elijah's command and with the striking of his cloak on the water. As they walked onward, Elijah asked Elisha, "Tell me what I may do for you, before I am taken from you" (2 Kings 2:9).

Elisha said, "Please let me inherit a double share of your spirit."

"You have asked a hard thing," Elijah responds in the next verse. "Yet, if you see me as I am being taken from you, it will be granted you; if not, it will not."

In order to get the double portion—the blessing of what was to come—the younger prophet had to witness his mentor leave, and let go. He had to be present in that moment of transition, present to the grief and pain. As 2 Kings 2 continues, Elisha cried out and tore his clothing when Elijah was taken up in a whirlwind by chariots of fire from heaven. Looking into the searing light, feeling the deep loss, he saw Elijah's cloak, his mantle, fall to the ground. Elisha picked it up, struck the Jordan River, and believed, as it parted, that the power and blessing of God had been reborn, passed on, and made new in him.

We may not like the idea of compost. It seems like an awful smelly idea. Elisha thought that Elijah's going away was an awful, painful idea. And yet, in and amongst the loss came a blessing—a double portion of his spirit.

The gospel, the good news, doesn't promise us a pretty garden with linear rows and predictable fruit. The gospel shows us a messier picture, but also a defiantly hopeful one. It is the gospel of the dust and the good news of the compost heap. It is not always pretty, it does not smell good, but it is always moving into the renewal of all things.

In founding and leading the Garden Church, I had to die to many of the ways I thought it could be, or would be. We didn't get the land we wanted, but then we got the space that turned out to be where life and need came together. People I'd been counting on left and funding fell through, but then others showed up and there was enough. I saw in myself and the community the utter mess that is death and resurrection happening at the same time, that which crumbles alongside the little sprouts coming out of the earth.

Each week as we gathered around the table—in the middle of an empty lot turned edible sanctuary, with the waft of an actual compost heap in the background—I saw the Divine Composter at work.

Our judgments softened and our hard shells cracked from being in community together. I felt my rigid ideas of "how it should go" and "what it should be like" get as mushy as an overripe banana as I stood with my arms lifted mid-communion consecration and waited for a gang of twenty-five-plus motorcycles to pass, or when we wove the sound of the fire sirens into the prayers of the people.

Rarely—no, never—did worship go exactly how I had planned. People didn't sit quietly and attentively. Albert would wander in, wearing his grubby white T-shirt, his baggy blue sweatpants, and his big sunglasses covering his puffy eyes. Some days he would doze through the sermon, but most days he'd have something to add. More often than not, he would loop around about some semi-pertinent fact of U.S. history, or replay a theological fact that he recalled from his religious childhood.

"Just two things, just two things, pastor," he'd say, and I would reply, "Not right now, Albert. Now is a time for listening."

But then, as annoyed as I often got in the mess, in the distractions, the interruptions, God would stir the dusty pieces of my heart. God would do her composting work, and by the time I stood at the communion table and looked up, I would see anew.

I would see the two guys in their twenties I hadn't met yet, next to Jimmy who lived out on the streets, sitting next to

Ed and Sarah and bubbly Leia and her green stuffed monkey, Mono Verde. Next to them was a downtown lawyer and then eighty-one-year-old Linda, a former nun turned ethnomusicologist, musician, cook, and farmer at the Garden Church. I saw the beautiful new thing God was creating in and amongst the mess.

I looked around as I chanted our well-worn communion prayer, "God speaks through outcast men, the pure and impure. God chooses what we despise to make us whole."

And God would turn over the compost in my heart.

Dottie would walk in just as we were gathering for communion with her white plastic compost bucket on one arm and a dish of rice and kale from the Friday farm stand on the other. "I should be working," she whispered to Nancy as she sat down, "but I just couldn't keep away. Besides, my compost was starting to smell," she said as she wrinkled her nose.

God was taking this big mess of all kinds of people who seemingly didn't belong together, and turning it into a beautiful church. This was the same God who had transformed Elisha's grief and pleading for a double portion of the blessing into fertile ground as a prophet among God's people. That same God was taking coffee grounds and slimy spinach and potato peels and turning them into nutrient-rich dirt in the back part of our lot.

Maybe it is no mistake that Christians press ash, dust, and dirt into each other's foreheads as we enter into Lent. We long for this symbol of death and mortality, endings and crumblings, because we know that within it is something deeply comforting. As we acknowledge that the endings are the stuff of which the new beginnings are made, we see that our dust is what makes soil for growth. The God that created us is the same God who is breathing into our dust, like what God did to primordial Adam, creating us anew. We are assured that even what is crumbling is being cared for. Love is infused at every stage.

In that moment, the dust dissolves what separates us, the ash burns through the illusion that we are anything but all in it together—immortal and human, creator and created, lover and beloved, dust, dirt, heart, and spirit.

We are all mixed together in the divine compost heap, where a new world is possible, renewed expressions of church can exist, and new life enters into our own lives. It's coming, and it is here, in and amongst that which is dying.

The following year, a core group of regulars who served on what we termed the leadership table met the night before Ash Wednesday. We feasted on dinner at Connie and Tim's and then gathered around their outdoor fireplace in the evening light for the burning of the palms. These palms had been carefully stored in the garage after Palm Sunday last year when they'd been waved with hallelujah shouts. The fronds had been cut from the palm tree in Tim and Connie's backyard, whose silhouette stood out in the moonlight.

As we watched the flames lap up the dried fronds, I thought about the cycle that we were experiencing: from the green palms waved to triumphal shouts of hallelujah to the palms laid at the tomb to the palms that provided a backdrop to the lilies at our Easter morning service.

Looking around the fire pit, I was overwhelmed by the beauty of the people who were here now. It was a year later and here were people I could count on and who were making this church their own. Linda, whose deep love and knowledge of liturgy delighted me and kept me on my toes. Bree, whose steady presence kept us organized and moving forward towards good. Jedi, who brought the unique perspective of a slightly awkward teenage boy and would always point us back to the reason we were there—to welcome all. My sister Nora, a music therapist with a great depth of knowledge and compassion for those who are struggling, and an intuitive sense of how music shapes our community. Nancy, forever connecting people and organizations like a pollinator bee. Peter, with his ability to make just about anything you could think of, from garden beds to artistically inked signs and a "Let's do it!" attitude. Annette, with her wise and artistic sensibilities, beloved and revered in the community, always looking for how she could serve. Connie, with her deep faith and constant love for everyone she met, and her interest in all aspects of the work. Her deep theological reflection was paired with her self-proclaimed title of "extreme food rescuer." Connie took leftover veggies—usually the ugliest ones—from the farm stand and brought them home to can, freeze, and cook into dishes she would bring back to the community for the Sunday meals. Her family had a sign in their front hall that read, "If you're looking for me, I'm in the garden." They were not referring to their backyard.

Each of these people on their own was a blessing; as a group, they were the foundation of the church. This was not necessarily the church I thought it was going to be, but the church that it was. In the warmth of this circle it was easy to see and accept how the ways I thought it was supposed to go had died and been transformed by God into the beauty of what had grown.

I thought about some of the hopes and programs I had thought would be essential; some of them just couldn't get off the ground, while others that I hadn't even considered a year ago were flourishing. I thought of the many, many people who had come through the gates of our garden lot, helped water or weed, promised to come back, but hadn't been seen again. But others stayed and were here around the table.

Knowing that God was holding it all in a loving cycle of embrace gave me the strength to show up to work each day. I think this was part of why Ash Wednesday brought me such comfort. It was a reminder of death and mortality, endings and crumblings. Within that, it was a comforting assurance that even the broken places, even the lists left undone and the endings of things that I thought were just beginnings, even those are held within God's loving embrace.

We took the ashes, carefully burned and sifted them, and mixed them with oil to take them again to the streets, streets that now felt familiar. Now it was a joy to share it with the next generation of leaders.

One such leader was Rev. Asher, a Lutheran pastor. We had connected through mutual colleagues and met in person when he and his partner moved to Long Beach. Not only did Asher *get* the Garden Church, he quickly became a pillar of the group, as his open-hearted personality became an integral part of the community. He delighted in holding chickens at our Earth Day expo, filled in preaching for me on occasion, and could always be counted on with his steady consistency and compassion when connecting with people.

The day after we prepared the ashes, Asher, Connie, Linda, Lisa, and I headed out the gates. Next door at the barbershop, a gruff, older, tattooed man grabbed Asher's hand as he walked by and then earnestly looked into his eyes as he received the ash. I watched Lisa bend over to have her face level to the man huddled by the bus stop beside the bench.

Linda followed along with us. Thanks to the many decades Linda had spent teaching and doing liturgy in the Catholic church, she was profoundly attuned to the power of ritual and was excited to extend it out onto the streets. As I chatted with a young couple near the crosswalk who were trying to under-stand Ash Wednesday and why we would be commemorating the idea of death, I turned to see Linda bending down to reach the forehead of a man in a wheelchair.

A few minutes later, now further down the street, we saw the man turn his wheelchair around and come back toward us. "Would you come to my house and give ashes to my mother? She really wants them, too." His words came slowly, deliberately. Asher and I readily agreed, and as we walked the six blocks or so to his house, we heard that he had moved here from Lebanon three years ago to join most of his family in San Pedro.

"We wanted to get ashes from church, but we couldn't because we weren't the right kind of Catholic." As we walked into their yard, past a tree overflowing with tangerines, his mother came out and welcomed us with a gentle embrace. Her son translated our words into Lebanese as we put the ashes on her forehead.

"Can we have some for the rest of the family for when they get home?" she asked as her son translated.

"Of course," we replied. The woman brought out a cot-ton swab and carefully took some sacred ash. They offered us tangerines straight from the tree. We ate them as we walked out, marveling at God in the ash, the vibrant orange of the tangerine peels, and the color of the bright blue February sky.

We walked by a young woman outside a dilapidated motor home, with all sorts of belongings lashed to the top. "Hey, they have ashes!" she called out into the little home, and four others came out. As I put ashes on her forehead, I saw behind her some dirty blankets and clothing hanging above the sink that looked like it hadn't had water flow through it in months.

We met up with Connie and Lisa and headed to the clinic across the street from San Pedro United Methodist, Lisa's church. The nurses and aides at the clinic jumped up when we arrived, called their coworkers, and then quickly fell in line at the counter.

"Thank you so much for coming for us! None of us will get off shift in time." Person after person started coming down the hallway for ashes.

"Can you do it really nicely, like you did hers?" one young woman asked.

"Okay, see if that's neat enough," I said with a smile, carefully pressing my thumb to her forehead.

We drove over to the local women's recovery home that both of our churches work with. "Thank you for coming here to us. Thank you for remembering us." Person after person, from the auto-body shop to the street corner to the art gallery. All connected. All human. All beloved. Dust to dust, dirt to dirt.

At the end of the day, Asher said, "Well, that will give me enough faith for at least another day."

When we open ourselves to spirit, to sacrament, and to our neighbor, God shows up. Those simple ashes, the stuff that compost and stars and humanity are made of, weave us back together again as we press them into each other's foreheads. We see those smudged crosses on each other and remember how we are all in it together—in this messy, dusty, beautiful, interconnected web of life. All beloved. All remembered.

-8-

REMEMBER ME

It was Palm Sunday at the Garden Church. Earlier in the afternoon, during worship, we had waved palm branches as we processed around our outdoor sanctuary. They were then laid on the ground at the entrance to the space, when a woman and her husband came in just as communion was wrapping up. The man was pushing her wheelchair, gently maneuvering it into the entrance of the sanctuary, completing our circle in time for me to come up to them and offer her the bread. "The bread of life," I said to her. She looked up at me with an open smile.

"Thank you," she replied in careful, slightly slurred speech.

After the final communion prayer, as we were singing our blessing song—"There is enough, there is enough, there is enough, enough and some to share"—the couple made their way with the rest of the community over to our food table. It was then that I found out that she had experienced a stroke and hadn't regained full control of her left side. As Lindsay attempted to get a plate, and then received the offer for help, she shared with me about her new teeth, that she could smile now, and about how much love she felt around the table.

When it was time to say goodbye, she took my hands in her hands. Her hand started to squeeze mine in return, tighter and tighter, and her face became panicked. She tried to get her husband's attention. Her brain and her hand were not communicating. She wasn't meaning to squeeze so hard.

Finally, with great concentration and a sharp exhale, her hand released mine and opened wide.

"Sorry, sorry, sorry," she said. "It's the stroke."

"It's okay, it's okay," I assured her. I rubbed her hands, hands that just a few days later would bless me with a profound act of love.

Four days later, we moved from Palm Sunday to coming around the table for Maundy Thursday, which celebrates Jesus' last supper where, hours before his arrest and crucifixion, he broke bread, passed wine, and washed his disciples' feet.

As a church community, this night felt right up our alley. We longed for a God who shared food and washed feet. In faithful, creative response, we had sent invitations into the neighborhood. Well, not *sent;* we gave them to everyone. Hand to hand, we passed them out, especially to our neighbors living outdoors, on the streets, people who may be offered food here and there, but were rarely given a gilded invitation reading, *You are cordially invited.*

We set up tables, blankets, and big pillows, low and cozy around the altar. We spread out white tablecloths, sprinkled bright flowers across the tables, and lit candles. Connie came in wearing her signature bright-colored patchwork baggy pants and bearing a mouth-watering platter of lamb. Annette arrived with a steamy vat of Croatian lamb called *cevapchichi*. Bread and fruit came next, then salad, and bitter herbs from the garden. We stood in anticipation, ready.

People started to arrive: a local seminarian with her twin four-year-old girls; Jarrett with his signature camo shorts; a young woman and her bubbly friend; an evangelical; a staunch Catholic; Annette with her cane; and a man still in construction clothing, straight from work.

Rev. Amanda, a Presbyterian church planter in the area, had graciously accepted my invitation, or maybe my pleading, to come help with the service, which had many moving pieces. As I stood in front of the colorful collection of people gathered, I was grateful not to be standing alone. Rev. Amanda was by my side, Nora was confidently leading music, and Bree was compassionately welcoming people, while simultaneously making sure there was enough food on each table, the water was hot, and everyone had what they needed. I saw Connie welcome Katie, and help her tuck her bags and sleeping roll under a bench before they sat down at a table together. I saw people sitting next to each other who I wouldn't expect to be communing. As I stood up to preach, the reality and beauty of the meal came into focus.

"We gather around the Maundy Thursday feast this evening to practice the *mandatum*: the mandate to love one another," I said. I explained that Jesus had first declared this mandate at the Last Supper, the Passover meal that has been celebrated over the centuries. The children of Israel, held as slaves in Egypt, first celebrated this meal on the eve before they crossed the Red Sea and escaped the tyrannical Pharaoh.

I preached that the Passover is a meal of invitation, liberation, and freedom. The lamb can remind us of the innocence God places within each one of us, the innocence that believes joy is possible, the innocence that can reach for freedom and hope despite the painful and hard things we've experienced. The bitter herbs remind us of the temptations, the struggles along the way—an inescapable part of the meal as well.

I opened up the sermon for conversation. People discussed the places where these stories came alive in their lives. One man spoke of his time in prison, and now being free but still feeling stuck. Another person talked about their difficult relationship with an adult child. Another reflected on when they felt imprisoned by loneliness. I stood back, letting the words and faces wash over me.

When the conversation began to slow, we brought out the bread and cup and remembered Jesus and his disciples celebrating Passover in Jerusalem, around that table in the upper room. It was during that meal that the Gospels recount Jesus taking the bread, blessing it, and breaking it, and saying, "This is my body, which is given for you. Do this in remembrance of me" (Luke 22:19). After supper, he did the same with the cup, saying, "This cup that is poured out for you is the new covenant in my blood" (v. 20).

I blessed the baskets of bread and the pitchers of grape juice; Amanda and Bree took them to each table and people passed them around. Murmurs of "The body of Christ, given for you" and "The bread of life, broken for you" filled the space.

During the Last Supper, Jesus took the embodiment of love a step further. He washed his disciples' feet. So we too got out the basins and carafes of hot water to show love to one another as Jesus had.

Then Amanda read about how Jesus, on his last evening with his disciples, poured water into a basin, washed his disciples' feet, and dried them. Afterwards, returning to the table, Jesus said to them, "Do you know what I have done to you? You call me Teacher and Lord—and you are right, for that is what I am. So if I, your Lord and Teacher, have washed your feet, you also ought to wash one another's feet" (John 13:12-14).

It was not until I looked out at my congregation's tattered flip-flops and cracked toenails that day that I remembered the genuine need embedded in this act of washing feet. Jesus washed his disciples' feet because they were dirty. Those women and men had been walking in sandals down the dusty Palestinian streets. Their feet were probably filthy. My congregation, as well, had not gone out to get Maundy Thursday pedicures in preparation for this service. Jesus washed his disciples' feet *because* they needed washing. As he did so, he instructed them, "I have set you an example, that you also should do as I have done to you" (v. 15). Jesus washed their feet not because of what they had accomplished, how they looked, or because they had earned it. No, Jesus bent down and washed his disciples' feet just because he loved them, as they were. Dirty toenails and all. Whole and messy, vulnerable and beautiful, loved, loved, loved.

That day, I shared a vulnerable story of my own—one about footwashing.

When I worked as a church outreach director in my twenties, I had a serious illness, I told them. For multiple months, I lay on my friends' couch, only able to walk tentatively to the bathroom and back. For this type-A, eldest child, independent-to-a-fault person, to be suddenly completely reliant on others was difficult. I could not do *anything* other than lie on the couch and receive care.

When Maundy Thursday came around, I had dragged myself to the service. It came time for footwashing and I sat there in the candlelight, waiting and wondering, "Who will wash my feet this year?" A familiar hand reached out to me. It was the pastor. But he was not just *our* pastor—my colleague, my dear friend—he was the person, along with his spouse and small children, who had been taking care of me during these months of illness. It was *his* couch I was lying on all day. He had been without a coworker for all these weeks, doing both his job and mine at church.

He had carefully poured the warm water over my feet. I was shown the love that is always available from God, no matter whether we feel we deserve it or not, and shown the love that Jesus invites us to show one another. Shown love when I felt I had been given enough and did not deserve more.

"We all have feet," I continued, looking around the circle in our dirt-floor sanctuary in the fading California light.

I talked about how we all have parts of our lives that have walked through the dust. Parts that are messy that we don't want to share with anyone. I reflected on how Maundy Thursday is an invitation to take off our shoes and socks, and say to another person, "Yup, I've got feet just like you. I've got parts of my life that aren't as pristine and put together as I would like them to be. I can't do it all by myself. I have to receive."

In her spiritual autobiography, *My Religion*, Helen Keller writes, "No matter from what angle [Jesus] started, He came back to this fact, that He entrusted the reconstruction of the world, not to wealth or caste or power or learning, but to the better instincts of the human race—to the nobler ideas and sentiments of people—to love, which is the mover of the will and the dynamic force of action."[1]

Jesus gives us the command to love one another, and then shows us what that looks like: humbling ourselves to each other, washing each other's feet, and yes, what might be the most difficult for many of us, being willing to have *our* feet washed. Receiving the expansive love of God and the reciprocal love of others means being vulnerable, admitting that we cannot live life by ourselves and we need others. And that isn't always easy. In fact, it makes us uncomfortable, exposed, and shy. Because really *seeing* each other, following Christ's example to love one another, is where it becomes real. The life of faith is not something that can be kept pristine, or something we just talk about or think about. Following Jesus' command to love one another means engaging with the messiness of life by helping others and letting them help us. This reciprocity is a reminder that we actually belong to each other, that when Jesus calls us to remember him, to love one another, it is a call to see each and every person as beloved and to acknowledge how the brokenness of the systems is a brokenness we are all part of.

As I heard more stories from our neighbors living on the streets and in their cars, I became more and more convinced that being unhoused is not a moral failure of the individual, it is a moral failure of society as a whole. As I struggled to find an apartment that I could afford, I also acutely felt the data that "over the past 30 years, rents have gone up faster than income in nearly every urban area of the country."[2] I met people who were working three jobs and trying to get by, and were, until that "last straw" happened. The rent was raised, the car broke down, an unexpected and uncovered medical bill came along, and the choice between rent and food, medical care and food, transportation to get to work and rent, didn't add up. Untreated medical issues, mental illnesses, and addiction were woven into many of their stories and exacerbated their ability to fight to stay housed.

When people ended up on the streets, I watched as their mental and physical health deteriorated quickly. One dear man, diagnosed with obsessive-compulsive disorder, was trying to survive in a tent, sleeping on the hard dirt, constantly checking his watch to make sure he got up and took the tent down before the morning police sweep, off his meds because he couldn't afford them, and refusing most food and water because he was worried about not having a place to use the bathroom. Predicaments like this had nothing to do with the moral or ethical fiber of these individuals, they were an indictment of our culture as a whole. Were we really "loving one another as Jesus loves us"?

Jesus called us to love, in tangible things, in things that we can touch, in things we can see in and amongst each other, called us to examine and repair the unjust, racist, and broken systems that continue to keep people in poverty. I wondered how my life would have been different had I not had friends and coworkers who had taken me into their home and cared for me when I was seriously ill. God is in the physical realities of being couch-ridden, of having dirty feet, of being hungry, and in a loving touch extended toward another. Or as Cornel West once said, "Justice is what *love* looks like in public."[3]

As I finished preaching, person after person came forward for footwashing. About half the people were unhoused or minimally housed, and hungry, and were excited about the fresh socks I had brought. I saw several new faces. One woman's twin four-year-olds insisted on both washing their mother's feet, with giggles and copious amounts of soap. Connie's husband, Tim, came after services at their Catholic church and joined his steady deep voice with Nora's as they sang, "Stay with me, remain here with me, watch and pray, watch and pray," as the footwashing continued.

I wondered at the vulnerability of giving and receiving love in this way as I stood back and watched the scene. This theme was showing up in my personal life as well as my professional life.

After spending much of my adult life single, I had met someone. Someone I might want to make a life with.

Six months earlier I had received a message from a friend who, after unsuccessfully trying to get me to attend a conference with her, had sent me a message from her flight home after the conference.

> Anna, I had a rather wild thought and I have no idea if you'd be interested, but for some reason I want you to meet a friend of mine who is a religious studies professor in upstate New York. His name is David and he is single and a very lovely and thoughtful guy. I hope you are not offended by my thinking of this, but I thought it would be great to e-introduce you two. I saw him at the conference this weekend and was reminded of this thought I had a while back about the pair of you. Am I nuts? (I never do this kind of thing.)

I responded that because being single and not wanting to be was awkward, as was online dating (especially as a pastor!), I welcomed her introduction. David and I began writing, then talking over video calls, and then booked flights and met each other in the middle: Colorado for a long weekend. We discovered that yes, indeed, the person we'd been talking with was someone we wanted to get to know better.

I hadn't yet shared this new tender possibility with my congregation, but as the relationship unfolded I found myself thinking about it more and more. We were talking every day and sharing our histories and stories, our hopes and dreams.

I was also learning how stuck I was in my independent ways. David was showing me love, and I was finding that receiving nurture and care was much harder for me than giving it. The "feeding and being fed" principle was easy for me—as long as I got to stay on the giving end. Now I was being given the opportunity to encounter my own resistance to being nurtured and cared for. I was being given the opportunity to be loved. Not just in a conceptual way, but in the nitty-gritty stuff of my life, the day-to-day things, including even my dirty feet.

The footwashing portion of the service was wrapping up. I was glad to see Lindsay and her husband back again after Palm Sunday. I went over to Lindsay.

"Can I wash your feet?" I asked.

She pointed to her laced up boots. "It takes so much time. Lacing."

I laughed, "Yes, I can see that. How about washing your hands instead?"

"Yes, yes!" she exclaimed. "My hands!"

Amanda was taking care of the handwashing station, so I asked her to bring it over. A few minutes later, as Amanda was drying Lindsay's hands, I heard Lindsay ask, "Can I wash yours?"

Amanda had already had her hands washed, but I hadn't. "Would you wash mine?" I asked.

Her face lit up. "Yes. I'll wash your hands." Her hands shook and seized. Amanda helped her hold the water. Lindsay took the soap and began gently washing my hands.

"What am I supposed to say?" she asked.

"You don't have to say anything," I responded.

"No, no, what am I supposed to say?" She insisted.

I realized she was remembering that, as we passed communion, we said the offering to each other. "You can say, 'This is how Jesus shows love,'" I said.

Lindsay nodded, and as she ever so gently rubbed the soap into my hands, she said, "This is how Jesus shows love. This is how Jesus shows love. This is how Jesus shows love." Oh so carefully, oh so lovingly, as she poured the water and dried between each finger, "This is how Jesus shows love."

-9-

BREAK BREAD, PASS CUP

Communion generally started for me early Sunday morning, while I was still in my pajamas, in my small kitchen. I would take a stick of butter from the refrigerator to soften, pull out the mixer and my favorite gluten-free baking mix, and get to work. The recipe became embedded in me. Sunday after Sunday, I mixed two-thirds of a cup of milk and one egg, added flour, and stirred. I learned gentle adjustments, like how many stirs resulted in flatter scones, and what consistency made the bread a bit bumpier and crisper. I'd plop the batter on parchment paper, making little round loaves in multiples of three—my nod to the Trinity, I suppose. Any extra dough after the communion bread was turned into morning breakfast scones as I added walnuts, craisins, candied ginger, and spices.

While they baked, I made tea and pulled up my sermon on my laptop. When the scones came out sixteen minutes later, I would grab one. It would crumble in my mouth as I reworked the sermon ending and finished reflecting on the message for the day. It often seemed that the sermons came back to bread, to feeding and being fed, back to the table where we find nourishment and belong to God and each other.

The first time I encountered this sacred meal, I was kneeling as the wine touched my lips, sharp and sweet to my inexperienced tongue. It mixed with the flaky bread, still fresh in my mouth. Jenny knelt too, right next to me. We were in middle school and inseparable best friends. Our mothers knelt beside us. The pastor's hands were weighty on my head as he blessed me with the words "May the Lord bless you and keep you." He spoke each word with reverence and a relaxed ministerial presence as he offered me my first taste of that bread and cup.

Since that moment, I have hungered for this sacred bread and blessed cup. The communion table became a place where I met God and found community—the gilded altar rail in the high-ceilinged cathedral in college, the summer camps in Colorado, the classroom where my seminary professor laid it out on the table. She had broken bread over our desks and passed around grape juice in Dixie cups. Moments before we had been fellow students; now we were gathered around the table together as the body of Christ.

The sacrament of the bread and the cup is shared throughout the Christian tradition. Along with baptism, it is found in almost every branch of the Christian tree, and is distinctive to the tradition, although it can also point us toward a broader connection to the human family and creation as a whole. We all have to eat. Food has the power to bring us together, to overcome the barriers that divide us, and to transform and heal us.

Yet food can also push people apart. The universal need to eat opens up the universal possibility for competition, selfishness, corruption, and power. When we look at food in our culture and the systems that support it, we see land fought over, people and soil exploited, food waste producing greenhouse gases, corporations swelling with ill-gotten excess, and people going hungry in the same town where half-eaten restaurant meals are thrown into a dumpster every night.

At the heart of this sacred meal, the bread is taken, blessed, and *broken*—a searing reminder that the very body of Christ suffered and was crucified. The church—Christ's body throughout time—is broken and wounded as well. At first glance, this might strike us as bad news, and yet in it there is deep redemption. What is broken is what makes us whole. Theologian Sheldon W. Sorge offers the invitation that the table "tells the truth" of this. "We live in a world today," he writes, "where baptism and proclamation are shared freely between major Christian communions that nevertheless remain divided at the Table. The Table tells the truth: the church remains sorely divided despite its hopes and claims otherwise."[1]

As churches and denominations, we are broken. We strive to create places of belonging, but we have simultaneously created places of pain. The stories of people harmed by church weighed heavily on me.

Christ was betrayed not just by the Roman Empire, but by his friends and followers. He knew what they would do, and yet he still gathered them to share his last supper. He gathered together a broken, human, fallible group of people and said, "Take, eat; this is my body" (Matthew 26:26). It was those people that he instituted as the church. The body of Christ, the church in its many forms on earth, is both broken and whole. Coming around the table can show us both.

When I first tasted that bread and wine I had no idea that the table would become the place where my call to ministry was clarified and formed, and the table would show the brokenness of the church and spur forward my call to serve at God's table where all are welcome.

In the years after college, I worked as a leader in a church where I could not stand beside my colleague, the pastor of our congregation, to serve communion to our community, because I was a woman. In that church, women cannot be ordained. I ached to break the bread and pour the wine for my community, telling the story of the Lord's feast with us, offering spiritual food and drink to the people I held so dear.

At the time, my pain and anger over being denied my place at the table confused me. I could not hear it for what it was: my very being shouting out my call to serve at the table. And not any table—the sacred table that was open to all. This call was not only about openness to who could receive, but also about a table where people were welcomed to serve based upon their calling, gifts, training, and ordination, not their gender or sexual orientation.

From that time of struggle and darkness, I continued to find the clarity, truth, love, and light of the claim that we are beloved and made in God's image, that I belong to God, and that I was called to serve at God's table.

After leaving that church and following the call to seminary and ordination, I began finding the power in giving—and receiving—this precious bread. I ate and offered the meal in a glass chapel on the California cliffs, on the moors of England, and in yurts in the woods outside Seattle. Years after experiences of exclusion, I stood in the Garden Church, remembered my own struggles, and hoped people would find belonging in community and healing around God's table.

The Garden Church shared communion every Sunday as part of our liturgy. Gathered on camp chairs and blankets, perched on benches and sitting on the outskirts of the circle, the community would come around the table. People who were mostly coming for dinner often arrived a little early, during the end of the worship service, finding themselves hungry for this bread of life as well.

As we greeted one another by passing the peace—extending hugs or handshakes and the words "Peace be with you"—I would quietly recruit someone to help serve communion. I always asked at the last minute, to encourage those who might overthink it if they were asked in advance. I wanted someone to follow the inspiration of the moment and hop up with a "Yes!"

During one particular week, Connie volunteered. She stood beside me and held the liturgy book as I raised my hands in blessing and chanted. "Jesus Christ is here and present through God's love, which binds us all together. The Spirit moves among us and burns away division and calls us to new life in one body."

Nora, sitting on the bench with her guitar perched on her legs, led the congregation in response. "Alleluia, alleluia, alleluia, alleluia."

I looked out across the circle, noting that Randy in his herringbone flat cap had taken his regular seat on the end of the bench near the entrance, smiling as two toddlers played on the blanket near the cedar stump table. "Creator of the universe," I continued, "you breathe in the darkness, bringing song out of silence, dance out of stillness, life out of death. You send messengers in every time and place, giving voice to your love. You speak through thirsty women, outcast men, the poor and impure. You choose what is despised to make us whole."

The *alleluia, alleluia, alleluia, alleluia* washed over me, and I took a deep breath and chanted: "A servant girl bears Jesus, your blessing, who turns the old world upside down. He abandons the temple, laughs at the powerful, kisses sinners and heals the unclean. He breathes out forgiveness, teaching us to walk in the way of compassion."[2]

The bread of life began to do its work as we invoked Jesus, the Christ, with and among us. Somehow it all held: the messy and broken, the beautiful and connected. As I reached down to lift up the bread, all would meld together into focus. This is the body of Christ, broken and whole. This group of people gathered is the body of Christ, broken and whole. I told the story of the Last Supper. "On the night before he was crucified, Jesus gathered together some of his closest friends to share the Passover meal together."

Picking up the bread and lifting it high so it could be seen from all over the garden, I continued, "Jesus took a loaf of bread, and after blessing it he broke it, gave it to the disciples, and said, 'Take, eat; this is my body'" (Matthew 26:26).

I lifted the cup and said, "Then he took a cup, and after giving thanks he gave it to them, saying, 'Drink from it, all of you; for this is my blood of the covenant, which is poured out for many for the forgiveness of sins'" (vv. 27-28).

Reaching my hands out over these ordinary, sacred things, I prayed, "Merciful God, we gather at your table in thanksgiving to share this sacred meal. Pour out your Spirit on us gathered here and on these gifts of bread and cup, and form us as one body, your human family. Heal us, free us, and give us your power that we may live as Jesus lives and love as Jesus loves."[3]

Each week it became clearer and clearer to me that this was not my table, not my bread. It was not up to me to decide who was worthy to receive this meal, or who was part of this body of Christ. This was not bread to be hoarded and controlled by the privileged. This was not the bread of our ancestors, available only to those of a certain sexual orientation or who were proper members of the church. This was not bread available to only a few. This was the bread of life. It was not my job to decide who could eat it; my only job was to lift up that bread and proclaim what was true: "Dear ones, this is God's table, so all are welcome here. All you need to be to eat here is to be hungry."

Connie put down the liturgy book and we picked up the bread and cup. We began working our way around the circle.

First to Rudy in his signature black T-shirt and black jeans. "Rudy," I said, "beloved child of God, the bread of life, broken for you." Rudy's struggle with mental illness was something he courageously spoke about, finding healing in being an advocate. Rudy had started coming to the Garden Church in the early months, then backed off, then returned, then backed off, then returned again. I later learned that he had felt badly about his ability to follow through on what he had offered to do to help, and he needed that continual assurance that he was welcome—regardless of what he had or hadn't done—to come around God's table.

Next I came to Peter, tall and lanky, with dark blond hair turning gray. He tucked his mandolin under his arm as he put out his hands, pen-stained from his architectural drafting work, and looked up at me. "Peter, beloved child of God, the body of Christ, given for you." Turning to his wife, Linda, who was sitting at the keyboard, I looked into her eyes. At eighty-one years old, a lifelong faithful Catholic, including fifteen years as a nun, she had no doubt received this bread more often than any of us. Her eyes were teary as she cupped her hands, one in the other, and lifted them up. "Linda, beloved child of God, the body of Christ, given for you."

I turned to the bench and looked into the eyes of my beloved, who was sitting there, in the Garden Church, in the flesh.

David and I had continued to talk daily and visit in person as often as we could over the spring and early summer. Now he was visiting me in LA for a month before he headed back to teach the fall semester in upstate New York.

David's visits so far had been during Open Garden time on Fridays and his predictably gentle and friendly presence was welcomed by the members of the community. Today was his first Sunday. It had been lovely to have someone to drive to church with and to have help setting up chairs, the front table, and the farm stand. His own faithfulness, and how he already loved the Garden Church and the power of spiritual community, continued to amaze and delight me.

As he looked up at me from the bench, I realized this was *a moment*: the first time I served him communion. "David, beloved child of God," I said. My voice softened, savoring the word "beloved"—not just by God, but by me as well.

I moved on to Nora, who had already roped David into joining the "choir section" on the bench. I looked into my sister's eyes and said, "Nora, beloved child of God, the bread of life, given for you." She often talked about how this was her one moment of "church" in the service; most of the service she was paying attention to the musical needs, anticipating what was next, and leading our messy group in song.

Also on the benches were two college students who had been coming for the past few weeks. Next were Jimmy and Jarrett and a friend of theirs I hadn't met before, all in a row with their sturdy tanned legs, combat boots, and surly looks. "Jimmy, beloved child of God . . . Jarrett, beloved child of God, the body of Christ given for you." As I turned to the third man, Jarrett tapped my arm with a whisper.

"Pastor, my friend's name is Phil." I smiled and thanked him for helping us to welcome his friend. "Phil, beloved child of God, the body of Christ given for you."

Bending down to a chair, I found Nancy, our networking queen. We had Nancy to thank for so many of the people who were involved, and the goodwill in the community towards our work. It was easy to say "Beloved child of God" to her. She looked up with a smile.

Next was a cluster of kids and parents on the blankets and chairs around the kids box. Etch A Sketches and books, paper and crayons were scattered on the blanket. Little Lydia and Christopher were here with friends, to show them their "outside church," as they called it.

In the early months of the Garden Church, my friend Rev. Nadia Bolz-Weber had posted about us online. The children's mother, Caroline, followed Nadia's work and the work of her church—House for All Sinners and Saints—in Denver.

Caroline was ecstatic that this new church start was a mere two miles from her family's house in San Pedro. Still happily committed to their Lutheran church, they began coming to the Garden Church in the afternoons, and often spent time on Fridays and Tuesdays for Little Sprouts and Open Garden. Caroline and I struck up a friendship; I was relieved and grateful to find someone who already *had* a pastor, but who *got* church and could also be my friend.

I squatted down to toddler Christopher first. "Christopher, beloved child of God, the body of Christ." Lydia stopped coloring and nudged her friends, bringing them both to attention. "Lydia, beloved child of God, the body of Christ," I said, and asked, "What's your friend's name?"

Completing the circle was my favorite part of communion because I would make my way out into the garden. Connie followed with the cup. We approached a couple sitting on the bench in the prayer garden and watching from a distance. "Beloved child of God." We found Sarah, who was following after toddling Leia. "Sarah, the bread of life, broken for you," I said as I handed her the bread. I knelt down, "The bread of life, broken for you, Leia."

"Mas! Mas!" Leia called after me, asking for more.

We walked up to a gruff, shy man sitting on the outskirts of the prayer garden, "The bread of life, broken for you," and then to faithful Karen, standing and greeting people at the front gate. "Karen, the bread of life, given for you."

I looked around and saw what beloved author Rachel Held Evans described as what God's kingdom looks like: "A bunch of outcasts and oddballs gathered at a table, not because they are rich or worthy or good, but because they are hungry, because they said yes. And there's always room for more."[4]

During the meal that evening, I introduced myself to Crystal, who had come for the first time that day. "Pastor, thank you for your words, I needed them," she said as tears welled up in her eyes. "I came because I was really, really hungry"—she pointed to her full plate of food—"but I guess I was hungry for something else too."

It was powerful to invite others to be part of serving communion with me. I especially loved serving communion with Connie. She got teary each time. The first time I asked her to help serve, she was nervous. "How do I do it? It's such an important job."

"Yes, it is an important job," I replied. "The most important thing you can do is to look each person in the eyes as you serve them and remember that they are a beloved child of God."

Once, as we came around the second side of the circle after serving everyone in the space, I took bread and looked Connie in the eyes and said, "Connie, beloved child of God, the body of Christ, given for you."

Then she took the bread, broke off a piece, looked me in the eyes through her purple-rimmed glasses and said, "Reverend Anna, beloved child of God, the body of Christ, given for you." In that moment, no matter what had happened before and after at church that day, I was fed.

One Sunday, a woman visiting for the first time came up to me and said that one of the most touching moments for her was at the end of communion when I had turned to Connie, who had been serving the cup, and *she* gave *me* the bread and cup. "It made me realize," our new friend said, "that it's about us all feeding each other, not about a one-way exchange from the priest."

Continuing to gather around the table changed me. Like the persistent wearing of the waves on the rocky shore, the table smoothed my rough edges. Sometimes the waves cracked me open, and I saw and felt differently than before. The table challenged me to look people in the eye and see them as beloved children of God—even the people that I was annoyed at and wanted to ignore. The person I got into a conflict with at the last meeting, the neighbor whose opinion I didn't appreciate, the congregation member who had been interrupting me all through the sermon to add in his own commentary—I was called to walk up to all of these people with an open hand and heart.

Albert had continued to annoy me for the past three months. His lack of impulse control—and *all* he had to say—were wearing on me, more than I wanted to admit. He kept coming back to church; I kept getting the opportunity to learn to love him. Some days he was very sleepy and easy to manage; others days he spoke at any chance.

A few of us talked it over and committed to working with Albert together as a group. We noticed that if he was told clearly, repeatedly, what we were doing, he could usually redirect his focus. "Right now is a time for listening," we might say. "Now we are going to sing together." "This is prayer time, not time to talk to each other about our prayers." "We're each going to take *one* turn to share. You had your turn, it's others' turn now." Albert's comments still frustrated me, and I found the constant redirection exhausting, but it was working bit by bit.

"Now is a time for sharing," I said after the sermon was done, and I rang the gong. I braced myself, knowing that sticking to my deeply held belief that God's word comes through more than just the preacher also meant opening things up to a speech by Albert. I saw him straighten up and, as he began to open his mouth, I reiterated, "What we're doing right now, Albert, is sharing about our experiences of light. Is that what you want to talk about?" He did want to speak about light.

Albert had once shared with Peter that he'd been officially kicked out of every church he had tried to be a part of. I was proud of our community. They were often much more graceful than I was. They just keep loving him. And me.

One evening as we were cleaning up, Connie said to me, "Albert really gets to you, doesn't he? But you know, one of the places I saw God today was when Albert shared so profoundly about light." I felt humbled and embarrassed by my own resistance to this work as my heart of stone continued to be worked into a heart of flesh. Connie had a way of calling me back to the work, back to our values, often by quoting me back to myself. "You taught me to look for the face of God in all people," she said, with a twinkle in her soft, brown eyes. "It's okay to change. If we don't change, we won't grow."

Being changed is uncomfortable. It demands feeling whatever feelings come up, be it grief or pain, connecting with our own suffering, or admitting that we were wrong in the past. It means stepping outside our comfort zone, exposing our own vulnerability. But the fact that we can change, that we are called to change, shows up at the table, too. Change is gospel. Throughout the gospel we hear the call: "Repent."

The Greek word is *metanoia*—to change our minds, to turn. In the Gospels we see people being called to change, and lives and relationships shifting as repentance takes root. I thank God for calling us back around the table, face to face with humanity, and continuing to call us to change, to be opened up.

One evening, after our closing circle, when we offered anointing and blessing for anyone who had life milestones (birthdays, anniversaries, days or months or years sober, new jobs), Frank pulled me aside with a sly smile. "Pastor, there was another milestone that we could have said during blessing, but I didn't think it was appropriate."

"What's that?" I asked.

"That Albert didn't say anything during the *entire* sermon. That's a first. That's a milestone."

"That's true, Frank, that's true," I said, doing everything in my power to keep a straight face and not let the laughter bubble out, alongside a deep growing affection for these men I got to pastor. A milestone indeed.

Even when it was not Sunday, I felt the power of the table, the stump in the middle of our sanctuary space, echoing its proclamation of being God's table where all are welcome to feed and be fed. I felt it on Thursday evenings, when the garden was filled with people enjoying the live music and mingling. I felt it on Fridays, when the garden beds were flooded with high school students learning about growing food, and when the group from Easterseals came and gardened and visited and sat happily in the shade. These things were not disconnected.

What happened around the communion table was integrally connected to the community meal that happened after, and gatherings throughout the week, and the work in the community as a whole. Every week, right after the final communion blessing, I would say, "We now move from our sacred meal to our shared community meal." The connection between the two was clear as the book of Matthew came alive while hungry people flooded the food table.

> For I was hungry and you gave me food, I was thirsty and you gave me something to drink, I was a stranger and you welcomed me, I was naked and you gave me clothing, I was sick and you took care of me, I was in prison and you visited me . . . just as you did it to one of the least of these who are members of my family, you did it to me. (Matthew 25:35-36, 40)

Jesus' words invite the reality that Christ embodied while walking on earth, showing us what following Jesus looks like: tiny mustard seeds and loaves of bread, bending down and washing feet, feeding and being fed. God is in all things and created us for a life of love and service. When we bend down and wash the feet of one whom we hesitate to even touch, we are serving God. When we take the bread, the wine, the water, God is with us. Cooking supper, writing poetry, wiping noses, digging in the dirt, all of these are love in action. As my late grandfather, Rev. Dr. Bill Woofenden, put it, "Love, by its very nature, must be doing something."

My early dreams for the church sought to integrate the natural and spiritual, individual and communal needs; we committed to working together for changed hearts and spirits in conjunction with addressing systemic injustice and working for changed physical lives. The spiritual and the natural work are interconnected. Jesus pointed to this reality when he equated one's eternal place with what one does for "the least of these who are members of God's family."

One Sunday, Katie cooked pasta sauce for dinner. Katie, her boyfriend, Tom, and their dog, Diana, were living on the streets. They had been living in her car, but lost it when parking fines piled up too high. Katie loved to cook and missed having a kitchen. The Sunday before, she was talking to Bree as Bree was passing around the sign-up sheet for cooking for our community meal. Katie found out from her that we had a Crock-Pot that could run off the solar panels. She asked if she could come to the garden on Friday and make a tomato pasta sauce. "Could someone else take the Crock-Pot home and keep it in their refrigerator until Sunday?" she wondered.

Bree came in Friday for Open Garden with a big grin on her face and got the Crock-Pot, a cutting board, and some spices she'd brought from home set up on a table in the shade. Katie was giddy with happiness as she cooked. Using fresh tomatoes, basil, oregano, and thyme from the garden, she chopped, stirred, sniffed, and tasted over the Crock-Pot.

"I love cooking!" Katie kept saying as she stirred. "Damn, I miss having a kitchen."

Farmer Lara offered to put the sauce in her refrigerator and heat it up Sunday. Lara overheard Katie mentioning that she would have liked to put some sausage in it, but couldn't afford to. On Saturday, Lara stopped at the grocery store for some sausage and added it. When she brought the sauce back on Sunday, heated and in the Crock-Pot, Katie made a few additional adjustments. It was ready to go when Linda arrived with pasta and parmesan cheese.

"This is a big, love-filled, community dish," Katie proclaimed.

"Communion continues," I thought as I watched her glowing face.

When people asked, "Is this a church, or is it a garden?" the answer was always yes. It was yes because we were about the transformation of mind, body, and spirit. We were about the transformation of earth, food, health, and community. They are inextricably intertwined.

Community and food are as connected in the Bible as they are in daily life. The book of Genesis opens in a garden, notes scholar Kendall Vanderslice in her book *We Will Feast*. In the garden, she writes,

> humanity receives her primary responsibility; to care for and tend the earth. The only restriction placed on those first humans was a restriction on what they could eat. God said to feast upon fruits from all the trees, so long as they stayed away from just the tree of knowledge of good and evil.

> But in God's love for the beloved creation, God calls it good, and in the narrative that continues through Jesus, humanity received a ministry of meals. Here, Jesus reconciled the relationships that were broken by the knowledge of evil. Reclaiming the cross from the sign of death to a gift and symbol of the continuation of life, Jesus asked his followers to do one thing: to eat. Through consuming bread and wine, Jesus gave his followers a way to again honor the interconnectedness of all creation.[5]

When we take this bread and drink this cup, we connect with each other. And when we break this bread and drink this cup, we connect with the faithful throughout time and geography—we connect with creation itself.

My friend Rev. Steve Blackmer is the priest at Church of the Woods in New Hampshire. For most of the year, he and his congregation worship outside on the eighty acres of land they are working to rehabilitate. They sing and pray and reflect on Scripture and creation together in the woods. Then, when they get to the time of eucharist, or communion, after the bread and the cup have been consecrated, they sprinkle some bread and pour some wine on the ground, offering it back to the earth. They are remembering their part in this great interconnected web of life.

Why did Christ lift up bread and say, "Do this in remembrance of me" (Luke 22:19)? Because Christ is present in all of this, and maybe especially in the simple and most essential things of life—what we eat. Communion has become a precious sacrament, served on silver plates and gilded chalices. Yet in its institution, Christ took up the two things most common, most basic, and most available: the bread and the cup. Surely at that Passover meal he could have picked up the traditional Passover lamb, or the bitter herbs. And yet he took that which people can—and have been able to—access and recreate over the centuries with many different ingredients and forms. Simple things of life made sacred. This bread from the earth—Christ's body. This fruit of the vine—Christ's blood. All connected, all intertwined, in the sacredness of all that God creates.

On Monday morning I pulled my purple hat over my unshowered hair and tied my walking shoes. Putting the left-over scones in a basket, I headed out to the nearby park to meet Caroline for a visit, while Lydia and Christopher played on the playground. Caroline and I sat on the bench and chatted about our training for a 5K race, and our mutual struggles to make life work in expensive Los Angeles.

Lydia ran over from the slides shouting, "I'm hungry! Can I have a snack?"

"Here Lydia," I responded, "I brought some scones."

Her eyes lit up. She reached out her hand. She chewed for a few moments and then turned back to me, "Pastor Anna, did you bring us some special prayer juice too?"

Beloved child of God, the body and blood of Christ, given for you.

-10-

IN THE SILENCE

In a community with a large Latinx population, Día de Muertos, or Day of the Dead, is a big deal. We did not know just how big it would be for our community until our second fall on 6th Street.

We had heard that the Día de Muertos street festival was going to expand that year to right outside our gates. There would be food, places for people to build family altars with photos and mementos for those who had died, booths of many kinds, and bands playing loudly. We decided to open our gates and invite people in. When we were planning, I suggested we get a chalkboard for people to write names of deceased loved ones, and we could pray for each one written on that board.

"We don't have time to get a chalkboard," Connie countered, "What if people just write on the brick wall?"

Out of necessity, I agreed. We walked over after the meeting and successfully chalked a few names onto the red bricks.

When we showed up on Sunday afternoon, hundreds of people in masks and face paint, marigolds and music, were already flooding the streets. As we opened the gates, they began to trickle in. People planted marigolds, the traditional flower of Día de Muertos, and wandered over to the art table to make paper marigolds. Small children hung pictures on the clothesline between the tomato plants, while their grandparents sat quietly in the prayer garden and watched it all.

At first people wandered in as if it were an extension of the festival, which in a way it was. Since they hadn't entered a building, it wasn't necessarily clear that they had entered a church. But with the invitation to write the name of a loved one who had died on the wall to be prayed for, or to plant a marigold for a loved one, the stories would start to flow from them, as would the realization that they were in a sanctuary, with space for naming the sacred.

Two young sisters came over to where I was standing by the picnic tables with tears on their faces. "We're so sad because of death," the older sister said. I asked if they had loved ones who had died, and they began pouring out stories about their cats and goldfish. I listened and nodded, and we talked about how it is hard to miss those we love. They wanted to take the pictures of their cats and hang them on the memories clothesline. Then they asked if there was any paper—"So we can make pictures of the fish." We dug through the shed together and found paper and colored pencils.

I invited them to take the paper and pencils to the picnic table, so others could also draw pictures of their loved ones as well, I said. By the end of the evening, the line was covered with colored pencil drawings representing all sorts of loved ones.

We had advertised that at four o'clock we would hold a prayer service and chant the names on the wall. When the hour came, however, there were a hundred and fifty people in the garden, and it was clear that they were not a captive audience. I downsized the liturgy in that moment. I stood, got everyone's attention, and pointed out the wall, naming it on the spot "The Wall of Remembrance." I let everyone know that we were going to start praying the names with chant and song. Linda taught the few listening to us the sung response. We invited people to join in, but most looked at us curiously and only a few came over. Linda, Nora, Tim, and I began anyway.

"Eugene and Jose and Mary and Enrique," I chanted.

"Come pray with us," Linda and a few others responded.

"Angelica and Sebastián and Grandma G."

"Come pray with us."

"Camila and Isabella and Nate."

"Come pray with us."

I stumbled over names, skipped ones that were illegible and surely mispronounced names left and right.

"Amy, and Gustavo, and Isabela and Elia Queen"

"Come pray with us."

"All you holy people"

"Come pray with us."

I made it through the first batch before my voice started to get scratchy. Linda picked up where I left off. "Javier and Rose and Grandma Lucy"

"Come pray with us."

I backed up to where Tim was standing, "Is this working?" I asked, fully expecting it was not, because there we were—four people being ridiculously religious in the middle of a street fair.

"Oh, yes, keep going," he said. "They're all watching." We kept chanting, up the wall and down the other side.

Over the next hour, the flood of people chalking names on the wall picked up. The word had gotten out. The wall drew weary souls who wanted to mark the names of their dead. Nancy and Annette came in after walking the block to encourage all the community members they knew to come join us.

Soon there were so many new names we started chanting again at five o'clock, and more people gathered round us. People were now following along as we chanted the names up and down the wall, and they scrambled to write the names of their loved ones before we got to their section. People were so intent on getting to the wall that they started climbing into the garden beds and trampling the vegetables. I asked Tim to keep an eye out and ask people to walk a bit further down to the wall where they could get to it without leaning over a garden bed. But scanning the crowd a few minutes later, I saw someone's big boots in and amongst the tangle of tomato vines. My first reaction was, "Why is that big, burly guy standing in the garden bed? Farmer Lara will be so upset." Then I looked closer. The man was drawing a heart around the name he'd written and was sobbing. Tim was standing by quietly. This was not the moment to ask him to move off the plants.

My friend Caroline and her husband, Jonathan, with their children, Lydia and Christopher, arrived at the garden. Jonathan and Lydia planted marigolds while Caroline and Christopher drew a picture. Then an older man walked in. I greeted him at the gate, and we chatted a bit. He was gruff. I couldn't tell if he was disapproving or just shy. He owned a business a few blocks down and was obviously well-connected in San Pedro. He seemed skeptical, and he hovered by the gate and looked around with furrowed brow. Eventually he said, "I used to garden a lot. I loved it, but I can't anymore because of my back." I acknowledged his sadness over this and said something about the containers by the picnic tables that were high enough for people to plant standing up or sitting in a wheelchair. He looked around again and said, "It's good to see the littles playing in the dirt." Then he paused, and his face shifted.

"My mother would have loved this," he said. "She was the president of the garden club. She died last month."

"Ooooo," I said, shifting my posture and face slightly, "I'm so sorry." He was silent. I asked him her name.

"Dolores," he said, his voice growing gruffer.

"You know," I offered, "what people are doing over there is planting in memory of people. One of the things we have are little rosemary plants for remembrance. We could plant one for your mom."

He nodded and grumbled something about his stiff back. "I can plant it for you," I offered, "if it would be hard for you to bend down to that garden bed."

"One of the littles, can they plant it?" he asked.

Lydia and Jonathan were still on the other side of the circle garden. "Hey, Lydia," I said, "I have a really important job for you. Would you be willing to come help?"

"Sure!" She bounced over.

We walked over to the man, and I asked if he'd tell her about his mom. I pointed them toward the Prayer Garden and left them to have the holy planting moment together.

Meanwhile Linda and I watched a ten-year-old kid write "ZACH" in huge red letters on the wall back near the corn and okra. The letters were so big and took up *too* much space,

I thought. "Now, that's more like tagging or graffiti," I whispered to Linda. "Do you think it's his own name?"

"Probably," she replied.

"I think we'll wash that one off after; it's not fitting with the tone—it takes over," I said, confident in my assessment.

I was about to pray the names, but the kid was still working on his name. I inserted myself. "So is that the name of someone who died?" I gently chided him. He will now tell me that his name is Zach, I thought. He looked me straight in the eyes.

"Yes, my brother," he said.

I paused, caught by my own false assumptions. "For Zach," I chanted, my voice catching. "Pray with us." Then to myself I said, Forgive me, Lord, forgive me. I prayed silently as I looked up at the giant memorial of love on the wall.

With live music coming in through the gates and a giant street fair all around us, it was an unlikely place to find the silence of the holy. But I was struck by the silence and the sacred moments in and amongst the noise and chaos of the city. I watched people silently writing names on the wall, bending down to dig and place their marigolds in the soil, quietly watching as their children drew the beloved family pet. The sacred was present. It was present in and amongst the chaos.

The presence of the sacred, the silence within the chaos and noise, was something we found and reminded ourselves of as we began worship each week. After taking the Bible, candle, water, bread, and cup out of the tabernacle basket, I would take out a singing bowl that I'd been given as a thank-you gift from friends years before. I shared about the difference between "quiet" and "silence." I invited people to listen to the many noises surrounding us in the outdoors in the middle of the city.

"I can promise you that it will not be quiet during worship today," I would say. "We worship amongst the wind and the sirens, cars going by and the occasional whirring of wings from the pesky garden beetles." But, I reminded everyone, even though it wouldn't be quiet during worship, we could still find silence, that sacred space where we can experience the presence of God. "Just as sometimes there is clatter and chaos in our heads," I said, "we can, amongst that clatter, bring our attention to the silence and invite a space for the still small voice to speak to us."

People shifted around in their chairs and nodded their heads, looking relieved that they were not alone in their trouble with stilling the barrage of thoughts. "I invite you to still your bodies," I'd say. "Sometimes you have to wiggle them before you can still them." I would demonstrate, shaking out my hands and arms and shoulders and planting my feet more purposefully on the ground as people shifted in their camp chairs and on the benches, and stretched out on the blankets on the ground. Nancy let out a soft, audible sigh as she arranged her frame in her favorite chair in the corner.

"Quiet your mind," I continued. "And open your heart to God's presence with us." I took the bowl, struck it, and ran the mallet around and around its rim as the sound echoed and grew. As the hum resonated out into the garden, I watched as people's bodies visibly relaxed and their faces opened up in peaceful expressions. This was my moment to breathe and take stock as well, letting the stresses of the past few hours of working together in the garden fade to the edges. I would pray for an awareness of the Holy Spirit there with us, and the ability to listen and be present to her guiding. We sat in silence together for a few minutes. I inwardly thanked my Quaker seminary for teaching me to be more comfortable with holding silent space. A motorcycle went by, revving its engine, the wind picked up and slapped the top of the shade tents against the frame, and the sound of the bowl continued to draw us back to that space of silence, encountering the sacred in this sanctuary.

I encountered the sacred in this organic sanctuary during worship on Sundays and on weekdays as well. The sacred seemed especially present when people were planting and caring for the plants with their hands, mixed with prayer in their hearts.

One Sunday a young man came in with his mom, who had been crying. "My dad died a few days ago," he shared with me in his limited English. "And we're so sad." I talked with his mom as he hovered behind her.

"Can we pray with you?" I asked. "And can we plant this rosemary bush in the prayer garden to remember him by?" They both nodded through tears.

I gathered everyone working in the garden, and we put our hands on the family's shoulders to pray. Then the son and I put our trowels into the earth and dug a hole for the little rosemary plant. "Can I get it some water?" he asked. I nodded and he poured water, mixed with tears, onto the plant.

Throughout the rest of that summer, the boy returned every week and watered the plant faithfully, sometimes on his own, sometimes with his mother, sometimes with a friend. Then the summer ended, and we stopped seeing him.

Two years later I was pulling weeds when two gangly teenagers came through the gates. "Do you know where the rosemary plants are?" I heard one of them asking Nancy, who was at the front gate.

"Hmm . . . I'm not sure," she replied and began to look around.

I looked up and recognized the teenager talking to Nancy. "The rosemary you planted for your dad?" I asked. His face lit up. "Yes, it's right over here," I responded. "Look how it's grown!"

At the following year's Día de Muertos celebration we added an activity: people were invited to take a bulb for a loved one and plant it in the circle bed that surrounded the sanctuary space. Jedi bustled around, handing out bulbs, showing people how to use the trowels, and directing planting spots. Little kids and their parents, shy young adults, and grandmothers took trowels to dig holes and then carefully pressed their bulbs into the soft, rich ground. The bulbs looked so withered and dead; the bulb scales, or leaves, on the outside flaked off like old wrinkled skin. Jedi explained how the planted bulbs would sit for months, covered over in the dark, kept warm in the earth and wet from watering. Then, one day, a green shoot would come up, followed by the stalk and buds, and then a beautiful gladiolus would blossom. "All of the plants here came from little, dead-looking seeds and bulbs we planted," he finished.

The gospel of John says, "Unless a grain of wheat falls into the earth and dies, it remains just a single grain; but if it dies, it bears much fruit" (John 12:24). While the Scripture is not exactly agriculturally accurate, I thought of it as I watched bulbs being planted that day, and regularly as Farmer Lara led

children, high schoolers, and many adult volunteers in planting hundreds of seeds throughout the late winter and spring.
We put those small, dead-looking things in the earth, assuming
that they would be watered and have sunshine and be cared
for. After six weeks or so, it was time to plant seedlings in
our sanctuary beds. Then, throughout the following months,
vegetables would appear, be harvested, and brought back to
the garden to be cooked into delicious dishes for people to eat
together at the community meal.

Each seed holds within it the potential for its life cycle. The
cycle is always moving and continuing, from being food to
the plant dying to the seed drying, being planted, and then life
pushing itself out of the seed as a new plant is born.

In order for that new life to grow, something has to be shed;
something has to die. That outer husk of the seed—the shell—
has to be broken through. It is in that process of shedding that
the new life, the plant—the resurrection—happens. Something
is left behind as something new is born.

The word *resurrection* has been formed within, and
informed by, the Christian tradition. There has always been
debate about Christ's resurrection—what it meant historically
to first-century people, how it developed as a doctrine in the
early church, and how contemporary Christians make sense of
it now. While the history of the word *resurrection* is directly
linked to the rising of Christ from the dead, the principle of
resurrection is universal: things need to die, to be shed, in
order for new life to emerge. Death does not have the final say;
new life from God is continually breathed into the universe.

This principle of resurrection is not a reason, or even a
method, to avoid the grief that life brings us. A concept of
life after death does not erase the reality of our struggles and

experience here and now when we face loss, transition, and pain. Instead, claiming the resurrection principle is claiming that the loving God of the universe is *in* all of it, with us, holding us closely, and working at every moment to bring healing and comfort, hope and wholeness, into our lives.

This applies to our internal deaths as well. We are not promised that being changed and engaging in the spiritual life is easy or painless, but God promises to be in it, continually making a new covenant and turning hearts of stone into hearts of flesh. Claiming the resurrection principle means that when we are in the middle of an internal struggle, we can ask, What are the things that I need to shed, to let die inside me, in order to receive the new life that God is calling forth in me? Be it the shedding of a belief system or the relinquishment of a habit that no longer serves us, we can trust that there is purpose and resurrection on the other side. With such trust, there can be a willingness to engage with the ambiguity of the unknown.

On a spiritual level, I hear this as a call to shed the husks of the things keeping us from experiencing honest connection with others, releasing the stories about ourselves that make us believe we are unlovable, and changing habits and patterns. Through the incarnation, God chose to be vulnerable and to make covenants of love with us. God put the very principles of the divine inside each of us. We may not usually think of God as vulnerable, yet Christ engaged in this universal principle of losing his life to gain it, bending down, and being a servant. Christ engaged earth and triumphed over human suffering through the ultimate act of opening himself to death and overcoming it through resurrection; we are left with the imprint of resurrection on our stories, in nature, and in our spiritual DNA.

When we lay the bulbs in the ground there is no sign of life whatsoever, but then, come spring, beautiful daffodils and gladiolus emerge from the soil. Death is not the final word.

One Thursday afternoon while sitting at a very long stoplight on Oceanside Boulevard, I received shocking news. Tracy, a friend and colleague from seminary, had died suddenly and unexpectedly that morning. I pulled my car over and parked in the lot next to the beach—frozen in disbelief and needing to know more. Through texts and Facebook messages, this impossible truth was confirmed—our young, vibrant, full-of-spirit-and-life friend had died that morning from complications while recovering from surgery.

I sat in my car. The light around me seemed different. The filter on life sharpened. My sensitivity to how precious and precarious life is was heightened. The line between life and death, the physical and the spiritual, thinned. How could someone so full of life be gone?

Tracy's death remained heavy on my heart when we gathered for church on Sunday. With the Day of the Dead happening on the streets, and All Saints' Day in our liturgy, we sought to welcome both traditions, traditions that have been celebrated through many generations as days to remember those who have gone before us. All Saints' Day is a day to celebrate the faithful departed, the great leaders of the faith—Mother Teresa, Saint Francis, Hildegard of Bingen, and Joan of Arc. It's a time to think of other saints in the world, ones who may not be formally recognized by the church, but are influential in our lives of faith—Martin Luther King Jr., Helen

Keller, Gandhi, Dorothy Day. It is also a time to remember those ordinary saints: those saints we knew and loved who have died, the ones we called Grandpa, Great-Aunt Gertrude, or Tracy.

Just after I quietly opened the gate and was starting to unpack the church basket, Lara came over from the tomato bed where she'd been working and squeezed my shoulder. "I'm so sorry about your friend," she said, giving me a hug.

In the gospel reading for All Saints' Day, we glimpse how Jesus responded to grief and death in the story of Lazarus. Lazarus was a good friend of Jesus. He and his sisters were part of Jesus' inner circle. Lazarus died while Jesus was out of town, and when Jesus arrived on the scene, he was met with Martha's words, "Lord, if you had been here, my brother would not have died" (John 11:21). Jesus saw Mary and Martha, the sisters, weeping and was deeply moved; he wept.

So often our response to death—be it of a loved one, another school shooting, or even the death of a part of ourselves that needed to transition—is to go straight to trying to fix the pain of loss, to make it better, to explain it away, to figure it out. We try to strategize how to never go through that kind of pain again, and we say things that aren't helpful as we reach to try to understand. Phrases like "She's in a better place now" or "That was part of God's plan" come out of our mouths, often causing those in pain to cry out, "Don't try to make it all better; death sucks and is sad and painful, and that's all there is to it!"

In the gospel text, we find Jesus grieving. Jesus weeps. Jesus takes time to feel, to acknowledge the loss, the pain, the life lived. And then, Jesus doesn't stop there—because while death is hard and sad and real and painful, the proclamation of God is that death is not the final word.

While the story of Lazarus may not feel comparable to our experience of suffering and loss, it invites us to question and wonder about the meaning of the text. Jesus doesn't go immediately to his friend's bedside when he learns he is sick. Jesus weeps—and then he raises Lazarus from the dead. And this miracle further prompts the Pharisees in their plot to kill Jesus. Yet through these complexities, Jesus' gospel message rings clear: Jesus says, "I am the resurrection and the life" (John 11:25). The expansive God of the universe, the incarnate God in Christ, is the resurrection and the life. God creates and animates our physical bodies, yes, but God has created more than that. The physicality of the body and this world is indeed infused with a spiritual reality, the spirit that goes beyond the physical, life that goes beyond death.

The Swedenborgian tradition has an extensive, well-textured theology about the afterlife and the nature of the natural and spiritual worlds. In his mystical and theological writings, Emanuel Swedenborg describes the afterlife as a vibrant, real place. Not "real" physically, but "real" in terms of the spirit: spirit goes beyond this physical life, this flesh and blood, and our loved ones live on in this realm. Swedenborg details the afterlife as a place where the truest parts of our inner natures show themselves, where we continue to learn and grow in being the people we were created to be. Heaven is a place where all different kinds of people are together— different faith paths and ideologies, different loves and ideas. The way of heaven is the beauty of variety. Maybe heaven is something like that feast described in Isaiah 25: a feast that the Lord prepares for us on the mountain, a feast of rich food, and well-aged wine, a table where God will destroy the shroud that is cast over all people, and will swallow up death forever, a garden sanctuary where the Lord God will wipe away the tears from our faces as we rest and feast in the embrace of God.

On the Thursday that Tracy died, I got out of my car, took off my shoes, and started walking down the beach. I walked and walked and walked. Perhaps I could walk off the reality of this loss if I just kept going. The sun was setting, and a family with little ones was playing in the waves. Gulls called out overhead. I looked out over the smog in the distance, tinged with golden rays. In that moment it was just so absolutely obvious to me that there must be something beyond this physical reality. Not because I need to prove heaven or make it all okay by assuring myself or others about what might come next. I knew and felt that there had to be something beyond this physical world because Tracy's spirit was so much brighter and lasting and shining than this earthly body could contain. I knew her spirit must live on, and that from God she came and to God she returned. This thought was the most peaceful, beautiful, achingly true thing in the moment.

I walked down to the water and took the water, as is my ritual—making the sign of the cross on my forehead, tracing the sign and words of my baptism. This time, the words that came were "From dust you have come and to dust you shall return." The ashes of Ash Wednesday and the waters of baptism, mixed with the salt of the ocean and the light of the setting sun.

-11-

SEEK THE PEACE OF THE CITY

We gathered around the whiteboard at our strategic planning retreat in January and wrote across the top, "Take it outside the gates." "It" meant the church, the vegetables, the community spirit, the feeding and being fed.

After our first few years of experimentation and growth, we had formed a leadership table, in addition to our legal board of directors, to more closely connect and represent the people who were showing up and making church together each week. The leadership table had met monthly throughout the fall and winter. When we arrived at our January retreat, people began voicing how they were feeling called to take the powerful mix of urban farm and justice-seeking in our community and heed Jeremiah's call to "seek the peace of the city" (Jeremiah 29:7 NKJV).

When it came time to plan for Holy Week, we took this whiteboard proclamation seriously as we created the liturgy for our community.

"How do we do the magic of Ash Wednesday in Holy Week?" Connie asked, sitting in my living room with a bowl of soup in her lap.

Willow looked quizzically at Connie and asked, "What does that mean? I wasn't there for Ash Wednesday."

Connie thought for a moment. "I think it's the chance to engage and interact with a stranger on the street in a meaningful way," she replied. "Often we just walk by people, but on Ash Wednesday you have something to give, something to offer, and so there's an opportunity for a different kind of interaction."

"What about flowers?" asked Willow's husband, Doug. "What if we had long-stemmed roses and handed them out around the neighborhood? Willow and I'd be happy to purchase them for everyone to distribute." Willow and Doug and their eight-year-old daughter, Terese, had begun attending the Garden Church soon after moving to the area earlier in the year. They had accepted my invitation to come for dinner and Holy Week planning at my place when I had seen them the Sunday before.

We read aloud each section of the gospel text for Holy Week and reflected on what we were hearing. Linda's voice gently read, "Mary Magdalene went and announced to the disciples, 'I have seen the Lord'; and she told them that he had said these things to her" (John 20:18), as we finished reading about Easter morning.

"Look, I drew the whole story!" Terese's head popped up from between her parents' chairs, and she showed us a detailed drawing of an empty cave, stick-figured Mary, and Jesus with glowing rays of sunshine radiating from his body.

The group of us debated lighting a traditional Easter fire on Holy Saturday, which brought up the matter of city codes and who had a fire pit. We divided up the making of lamb, bread, salad, and fruit for our Maundy Thursday meal.

"This feels like Holy Week already," Annette said. "Here we are, as a community, reading the Scriptures, and they are coming alive."

A month later, I arrived at the garden on Palm Sunday to see big palm branches cut from Connie and Tim's backyard. They were placed next to a stack of smaller branches that Nora and I had cut from the palm bush by the front gate—it was the one and only plant that had been in the garden before us, and was now thriving thanks to water and regular trimming. We set up the picnic table with big sheets of cardboard, markers, and a collection of scriptural quotes that captured the world we were longing for and working towards.

"For I was a stranger and you welcomed me."

"We will seek the peace of the city."

"Love your neighbor as yourself."

"Feed the hungry."

People arrived for Work Together time and started planting new green bean starts. We invited others to come make signs with us. Peter's skilled architectural hand scripted, "We will build homes and live in them; plant gardens and eat their fruit." Asher wrote the words of Isaiah 2:4 in big block script: "They shall beat their swords into plowshares." Asher had been attending the Garden Church more and more frequently in the afternoons after attending the local Lutheran church in the morning. Connie came over with a new friend from the streets.

She introduced us to a tall man in a slender pink dress and an equally pink wig.

"Welcome!" Asher said "Want to make a sign to pray for the changes you want to see in our community?" The man nodded and began quietly looking through the quotes until he found the right one: "Blessed are those who mourn, for they will be comforted" (Matthew 5:4).

"That's what we need," he said, as he began writing it on his sign.

As we gathered to worship, Nora's voice rang out, calling people together with song. A crowd gathered, adults and children, young and old. After we sang and unpacked the tabernacle, our church in a basket, Nancy offered to read the gospel passage. She stood, all five-foot-one-inch of her, to read the story of Jesus coming into Jerusalem on a donkey while crowds laid down branches and their cloaks and coats, crying "Hosanna," which means "Save us!" They were hoping for a change in the power systems in their world.

Asher and I had discussed the story earlier in the week. As we batted ideas back and forth, the Palm Sunday procession began to take on the look of a protest in our minds. "It's like . . . if Jesus was some homeless Middle Eastern dude riding his bike down Wall Street or marching into Washington, D.C., the day after the inauguration with a crowd of tens of thousands wearing pink hats," he mused.

I had invited Asher to preach with me that Sunday, and we shared the sermon back and forth. I described what were probably two distinct processions happening that day in Jerusalem. Pilate's procession held pomp and opulence, showing off the power, violence, and prestige of the empire. Jesus' procession, in contrast, offered an alternative vision: a world where the poor are lifted up, the sick are healed, and the hungry are fed. Asher then described what Jesus showing up with this alternative vision might have looked like. I concluded the sermon with an invitation to think about what this world is that we're longing for, praying for, and working for: a world where the lion and lamb lie down together.

After the sermon, people picked up palm branches, ribbons, and signs and formed a procession. I led with a large metal Ethiopian cross held high in one hand and a palm branch in the other.

I sang out the words of Revelation 21:4: "God will wipe every tear from their eyes."

Linda struck the gong and led the line of people singing, "Hosanna, hosanna, hosanna!"

We walked out the gate, turned right, and headed down the sidewalk.

I called out the familiar words from Matthew 25: "I was a stranger and you welcomed me."

"Hosanna, hosanna, hosanna!"

We sang as we walked past the dry cleaner's, the independent raw juice shop, the empty storefronts, and around the corner shop.

"What does the Lord require of you but to do justice, and to love kindness, and to walk humbly with your God?" I sang out the words of Micah 6:8.

As we sang the *hosannas*, a few cars slowed and rolled down their windows to listen. "Hosanna!" one passenger called out.

We continued down the next side of the block and turned the corner to head towards our back parking lot.

We called out the commandment from Mark 12:31: "Love your neighbor as yourself!"

"Hosanna, hosanna, hosanna!"

As we walked under tall apartment buildings, someone called out from the third floor window, "We love the Garden Church!"

I smiled and felt a rush of gratification. We waved our palms and signs up toward the voice as we turned and marched through the parking lot and into the back gate.

We ended with the charge from Jeremiah 29:7: "Seek the peace of the city."

"Hosanna, hosanna, hosanna!"

On the Wednesday of Holy Week, my friend and mentor Sara Miles flew down from San Francisco to spend Holy Week with us at the Garden Church. Earlier that year, after years attending St. Gregory of Nyssa Episcopal Church, founding the Food Pantry, and spending a decade on staff, she had retired. This was her first Holy Week not on staff at a church in many years, and I had invited her to join us. She said that would be just the thing to ease the transition.

It was ambitious, but that year we had decided to hold services for Good Friday and Holy Saturday, as well as Palm Sunday, Maundy Thursday, and Easter Sunday. I was delighted that Sara would be joining us.

I picked Sara up at the airport and we ran errands on the way home. "I saved the stop at the Croatian butcher shop until you were with me," I said. "Because I knew you wouldn't want to miss it." We walked through the swinging door in the strip mall and I responded to the friendly greeting from Darko behind the counter. Several people were in line, which gave us time to poke around and point out the egg noodles, spices, sauces, and hard candies we'd never heard of.

"Next!" Darko's son called out. I stepped up to the counter to order a medium-sized leg of lamb, some ground beef, and "Some *chivachipee*?" Even after three years of ordering this delicious lamb sausage, I still was not pronouncing it properly.

"Almost!" He laughed. "*Cevapchichi*," he corrected. "Put the emphasis on the *ch*'s." We left with a big bag of meat along with a bag of ground coffee, much to Sara's liking.

"Before we go home, can we drive by the church?" she asked. "The last time I saw it in person was the month before you opened the gates." We pulled up along 6th Street and lucked out with a spot out front.

Sara had come down for a Sunday gathering just weeks before we had opened on 6th Street, and was there with me the day I had signed the lease for the lot. After the anticlimactic lease signing (didn't our landlords know how exciting this all was?), we had walked across the street to these tall green gates that were now so familiar, anointed them, and prayed over them and the space, naming it as sacred, naming it as a church.

"Wow, Anna, just wow," Sara marveled as I unlocked the front gate. "Look at that church." I showed off the new garden beds. Soon we were talking through where the tables would go the next night for Maundy Thursday, and where to put the fire pit for the Easter Saturday vigil.

The next afternoon we loaded up the back of my Honda Fit with tubs of towels and washcloths, dishpans for footwashing, two big totes filled with the fancy white tablecloths, and a pile of water pitchers. When we arrived, Bree, Linda, and Peter were moving tables and tidying up the front garden beds. Connie showed up soon after with serving platters and three big bags of new socks we'd been collecting for people to have after the footwashing. Tim would bring the food shortly before the service.

Everyone worked to set up tables around the altar and put on the white tablecloths and electric candles that wouldn't blow out in the wind.

Everything was ready before six o'clock. Asher suddenly appeared at the gate. "Asher!" I exclaimed. "I didn't think you were going to be able to join us tonight."

"I was planning on attending another service," he said, "but I kept thinking of you and Sara and the Garden Church and washing feet with this community and I just couldn't keep away." I introduced Asher and Sara and they gave each other a big hug. "I feel like we know each other because we have some of our favorite people in common," Asher declared.

Sara and I huddled around the notebook with the text of the service in it. I insisted that Asher join in.

As in the year before, the tables were filled with all kinds of people who wouldn't usually hang out together, eating, sharing, and passing each other lamb and bread and fruit. Sara and Asher stood on either side of me as we took turns chanting the communion prayers. Sara's low, rich voice on my left and Asher's sweet tenor on my right rose in a steady hum as I chanted the blessings over the bread and cup.

Lord Jesus Christ,

Present with us now,
As we do in this place what you did in an upstairs room,
Breathe your Spirit upon us and upon this bread and cup,
That they may be heaven's food and drink for us,
Renewing, sustaining and making us whole,
And that we may be your body on earth,
Loving and caring in the world.[1]

We took the bread and cups to each table and watched as Annette was served by her precious husband of forty-three years. Annette then turned and served it to Octavia, who then shared it with Katie and her boyfriend, Tom. Randy and Jarrett turned towards each other and shared this sacred meal. Nora and two of her friends from work passed the cup to little Terese, who then passed it to her mother.

As we moved into footwashing, I watched Terese lovingly wash her mother's feet and express audible delight while putting new polka dot socks on her after the feet were dry. At the other station, I saw Tom bending down and carefully washing his girlfriend Katie's dirty feet. They had been through so much this year: losing jobs and homes and cars and health, and yet, somehow in that moment all that mattered was that they could still express their love to each other. Their dog, Diana, tried to lap up some of the soapy water, and they laughed. Bree jumped up and took Diana over to the water trough for a drink.

Connie was washing Sara's feet—Connie, having read Sara's books and followed her work, looked up to Sara with awe. In washing her feet, she got to find out that Sara was beautiful and human, just like everyone else. Connie then took off her brown boots, which she kept in her car for Garden days, after ruining one too many pairs of tennis shoes. I caught her eye as she glanced around, wondering who would wash her feet. I went over, knelt down, and began to pour warm water over her toes.

All the feet and hands were washed. We blessed the gathered congregation and, while quietly singing, took the basins of water over to the prayer garden.

Sara gently spoke Jesus' words from John 13.

> Now the Son of Man has been glorified, and God has been glorified in him. If God has been glorified in him, God will also glorify him in himself and will glorify him at once. Little children, I am with you only a little longer. You will look for me; and as I said to the Jews so now I say to you, "Where I am going, you cannot come." I give you a new commandment, that you love one another. Just as I have loved you, you also should love one another. By this everyone will know that you are my disciples, if you have love for one another." (vv. 31-35)

We poured the water over the rosemary bushes and quietly made our way out into the dark of the Maundy Thursday night.

The next evening, after a long hot Friday in the garden, a quick walk, and an early dinner, Sara and I were back around the altar. Pastor Lisa and some of her congregation from the San Pedro Methodist Church joined us, as did much of Connie and Tim's out-of-town family. Terese, Willow, and Doug showed up with three huge bunches of daisies.

People came in soberly as Peter played his mandolin and Linda began singing, "Were you there when they crucified my Lord?" We prepared to walk the Stations of the Cross, honoring the ancient church tradition of fourteen images with readings and prayer that retrace Jesus' journey to the cross. While the stations are often depicted in churches and cathedrals with carvings, paintings, or other art around the sanctuary, we were preparing to walk them around our block.

Sara led people to the prayer garden, and called out the first station: "Jesus prays in the garden."

Peter's voice rang out over the group, reading the words of Jesus as he was in the Garden of Gethsemane. A few more people from the Methodist congregation came in through the gates. Pastor Lisa beckoned them over.

Peter concluded with the text from Mark 14:37-38. "He came and found them sleeping; and he said to Peter, 'Simon, are you asleep? Could you not keep awake one hour? Keep awake and pray that you may not come into the time of trial; the spirit indeed is willing, but the flesh is weak.'"

I rang the gong, and Asher prayed, "Lord, grant us strength, that we may seek to follow your will in all things."

As we began moving out the gate, Linda led us in singing "Kyrie Eleison," which means "Lord, have mercy."

We stopped outside our front gate for the second station. Connie and Tim's daughter-in-law read the next passage, outlining Judas's actions and the beginning of his betrayal of Jesus. Lisa prayed, "Lord, grant us courage that our lives may not betray your love."

Terese had offered to carry the icon banner of the crucified Christ, a print of the icon that our dear friend Paul Fromberg, the rector at St. Gregory of Nyssa, had created. She walked in front with me as I held the big metal Ethiopian cross high in my hand, and we made our way down 6th Street. We stopped halfway to the corner in front of the leather goods store for the next station, rang the gong, read, and sang "Kyrie" to the corner.

A few people had begun to follow us, and others approached us here and there. People in the procession handed them white daisies and invited them to join in. Some began walking with us, and others made their way back into the streets, daisy blessing in hand. An older man in a car opened his window to receive a daisy and drove quietly alongside us.

With each stop and each reading, I felt the weight of the story settling on us. I noticed the places of brokenness and the struggle in the neighborhood. We turned the next corner. The apartment building where the Garden Church cheerleader had called out from the window on Palm Sunday was now dark. The street was quiet.

The gong broke the silence. Willow read the wrenching tale of Peter's denial of Jesus, concluding with, "Then Peter remembered what Jesus had said: 'Before the cock crows, you will deny me three times.' And he went out and wept bitterly" (Matthew 26:75).

We paused for a long, silent breath, and heard sirens in the distance. A mother pushing a dilapidated stroller with a fussing toddler in it emerged from the alley and looked at us warily as she continued walking.

"Lord, grant us honesty that we may never fear to speak the truth," Sara prayed. We continued down the street with the mournful "Kyrie" on our lips.

Bree's voice rang out the chief priest and guards' call to crucify Jesus as she looked around at this street that she had come to care for so deeply, and for the people whom she saw being crucified by the lack of healthcare and housing, by addiction and untreated mental illnesses. Someone quietly read, "Then

Jesus said, 'Father, forgive them; for they do not know what they are doing'" (Luke 23:34).

As we rounded the block from 7th Street onto busy Pacific Avenue, I noticed how many of the shops on this stretch of road were boarded up. I was usually driving past or walking quickly on my way somewhere; I hadn't really taken in the death of the businesses on this block and the black shrouds of painted plywood in the windows. The strain between revitalization and gentrification continued as businesses came and went and the focus on the area ebbed and flowed.

We moved to the corner of Pacific and 6th, and Connie's daughter narrated the last words of Jesus from Luke 23:46: "'Father, into your hands I commend my spirit.' Having said this, he breathed his last." Her voice cracked as she read the last word, and she reached out to squeeze her wife's hand.

I waited for a long and deep pause before praying, "Lord, into your hands we commend our spirit."

We bowed our heads as the light turned green and a stream of cars revved their engines as they passed. We made our way back to our gates on 6th Street.

Willow read about Joseph of Arimathea taking Jesus' body, wrapping it in clean linen, and laying it in a tomb. Sara, Terese, and I took the crucifixion banner and laid it over the altar with the cross I'd been carrying on top of it. Sara invited us to lay our flowers on the icon. One by one, the congregation came forward and laid their offering of remembrance on the altar.

When almost everyone was gone, we placed the icon in the tabernacle and left the flowers around the altar for the next day. It felt holy to mark the brokenness, death, and pain in the community; each of those flowers held vigil for us, in the middle of the city. With the image of the stone being rolled over the tomb fresh in our minds, we locked the back gate on our way out.

⟡⟡⟡⟡⟡⟡⟡

Holy Saturday started out slowly. Before it got too hot, Sara and I put on our hiking shoes and went to one of my favorite spots—a walk out along the cliffs. We wound our way through tangles of bougainvillea and past a mobile home park, and then the path opened up on a spectacular view across the channel to Catalina Island.

As we walked, I shared with Sara all the conflicted thoughts and feelings swirling about what my relationship with David, to whom I was thrilled to now be engaged, would mean for my work at the church. I was so grateful that David and I had found each other after all these years; he was someone I wanted to do life with and have a family with. But it was hard trying to figure out how to integrate two careers and a cross-country relationship.

"On the one hand, it's a no-brainer," I said. "I love him, he loves me, and either of us are willing and ready to uproot and move so we can be with each other and spend the rest of our lives together."

"Right," she replied.

"But, it's also ridiculously complicated." I sighed. "The thing is, at this point it feels like we just have to be practical. For David, finding a job as a religious studies professor is so hard, and it turns out being a minister is actually much more flexible. But damn, Sara, it's so hard to even consider leaving the Garden Church only a few years in."

"Yes," she said. "But they're going to be fine without you."

"Really?" I asked. "Are you sure?"

"I'm sure," she replied. "And you've always known you weren't going to be here forever. Your call was to plant this church, not to pastor it forever. You knew this going in and you've been clear about it throughout."

"I know, it's just really hard to think about actually leaving. I love them, you know."

"I know," she replied, "I know."

We kept walking along the cliffs, hugging the fence where the areas of erosion felt too close, until the trail brought us to a hillside covered in vibrant mustard bushes. We went silent, taking it in. "The kingdom of God is like . . . ," Sara said quietly, quoting Matthew 13:31.

As we gathered that evening, the sanctuary held a fire pit for the first time, for the Easter fire. Sara spread the crucifixion banner on the altar and covered it once again with everyone's flower offerings. Linda brought back the big paschal candle, fully decorated, in the tall, windproof lantern I had bought for it.

Willow, Doug, and Terese walked in with a gorgeous three-tiered tray of chocolate-dipped strawberries and fancy makings for s'mores. "To roast in the campfire!" Terese exclaimed, her brown hair swaying as she ran forward to wrap her arms around my waist for a hug.

A while later we rang the gong and the small group gathered together. A few men whom we hadn't met before but who frequented the coffee shop down the street came, sitting on one of the benches with several regulars who were already there. Brad, with his dog, Millie, sat on the bench in the prayer garden.

I welcomed everyone to our Easter vigil. "This is the night in which our Christ passed over from death to life," I said. "We gather to listen to the record of God's work in history, recalling how she kept faith with her people in ages past, and came as Jesus Christ to be our redeemer. This is the Passover of the Lord! We will share in the victory of resurrection over death."[2]

We sang as the paschal candle was lit. Then Linda stood up and joined me, singing lines from the Exsultet, the Easter proclamation. I watched the faces around the circle track the story as the ancient words that have been chanted by the faithful for generations took up residence around our paschal candle's holy flame.

Then, readers theater style, we read the Scriptures for the evening's vigil, starting with Genesis and the creation story, which Willow and Octavia read together. Octavia's rich tones boomed out the voice of God. Brad's dog, Millie, who rarely barked, barked and yelped, accenting the creation of animals and making us all laugh as she seemed to know it was her turn to participate. Rev. Asher read the psalm and passed the book to Linda, who read the story of the exodus and the children of Israel escaping the tyrant Pharaoh. We ended with a text from Isaiah.

> Ho, everyone who thirsts,
>   come to the waters;
> and you that have no money,
>   come, buy and eat!
> Come, buy wine and milk
>   without money and without price. . . .
>   Listen, so that you may live.

I will make with you an everlasting covenant . . .
you shall go out in joy,
    and be led back in peace. (Isaiah 55:1, 3, 12)

Nora rose and began to sing the gospel. The hair stood on my arms as she recounted Mary Magdalene and Mary the mother of James and Salome going to the tomb to anoint Jesus and finding him gone. As her voice rose and fell, a quiet came over the garden and seemingly over the whole city. All creation was pausing to honor the risen Christ. As the last notes landed, "The gospel of our Lord, praise to you, Lord Christ," we released a collective sigh. Praise to you, Lord Christ, indeed.

With that, Easter had arrived. We all stood as the solemn silence shifted to relief and joy that Christ has risen and was there with us. We made our way to the gates for the final reading, the Resurrection Sermon of St. John Chrysostom. I had asked Brad, who lived in a tent in the neighborhood and had a booming voice, if he would read it. Brad wasn't sure about the idea, so I asked if he and Peter could read it together. The two of them had struck up a friendship as they built new garden beds a few months earlier and had been meeting for breakfast at a local diner every couple of weeks. Peter and Brad had practiced the reading and figured out who would read what part. Brad had been sitting on the edge of the sanctuary through most of the vigil—Millie's barking gave him a good excuse to listen from a distance. But now he came up and joined the group at the gate. As we all faced out to the street, Peter began,

If there are devout and God-loving people here;
    welcome to this beautiful, radiant feast.
If there are any careful servants of God,
    come and rejoice with the Lord.

If anyone here is worn out from fasting,
    tonight you will get your fill.

Brad took over as Millie strained on her leash.

If you've been working from the break of day,
    tonight you will be paid in full.
If anyone came to work in the morning,
    the thanksgiving meal is spread for you.
If any of you showed up in time for lunch,
    don't worry, there is plenty for everyone.
If some of you could only manage to come in the afternoon,
    you haven't lost out on anything.
If anyone came right before closing time,
    don't give it a second thought, you're right on time!

Peter's voice wove back in as he looked up and down the street, calling out to the guys across the street in the alley and the grandmother and granddaughter walking by.

The Founder of the Feast is gracious;
    the last one in gets as much as the first.
God is compassionate with the last as well as the first;
She gives freely to all.
So, everybody—enter into the joy of our Lord:
    newcomers and old friends, share the bounty.
Rich folks and poor: everyone celebrates together.
Sober or shabby, God honors you both.
Those who fasted, and those who did not, rejoice today!
The table is full of rich foods; no one goes away hungry.
Everyone is welcome to the banquet of faith;
God's goodness is freely given to all.

As Brad and Peter read, I thought about the first day Brad had come in through the gates when the Garden Church was first beginning. Until that day we'd known him as the guy who occasionally walked by with a big dog, obviously drunk and slurring insults at us. I usually responded with a wave and a smile. Occasionally, I would meet him on the sidewalk earlier in the day and we would exchange more pleasant greetings, but he never came in. Sometimes he stood outside the gates, but he still didn't come in. Until one Sunday. He came in halfway through worship, staying near the gate, received communion when I offered it, then left. The next week he came a little earlier and stayed a little longer. The next week he stayed even longer.

A few months after his first time in the garden, Brad stopped by on a Saturday as we were getting ready for an event with some out-of-town guests. He told me he was on his way to the bar, and I invited him to stay. He sat on the prayer garden bench for a while, Millie beside him. A few people sat and talked with him.

Eventually, it was time to give the visiting group a tour of the garden. I pointed out the different spots and explained what happened in each one. When we got to the gates, I talked about how all kinds of people came through the gates. "Like Brad," I said. I asked if he'd like to share his story with our visitors, not knowing what he'd say.

"I used to walk by this place all the time and all I would do is heckle them," he began. "But then, one Sunday, I saw you all here, singing, and thought, 'There is this circle of people, being peaceful together,' so I came in." Brad talked about how the community had embraced him and how he felt a part of it. "Reverend Anna and this community just love people up," he said.

I knew Brad was reluctant to come back at times, and at times he had conflicts with us, but he had friendships with some of us too. He had said he would come and read on this

Easter Saturday, and here he was, standing up and shouting out in his loud voice, his big curly hair making him look even taller than he was.

> No one has to mourn tonight,
>> for God brings everyone into his embrace.
> Death thought it had beaten him down,
>> but our Savior beat death.
> He stripped death of its power
>> when he took death on himself.
>
> Death tried to swallow him up, but it gagged on his life.
> Death swallowed a body and choked on God.
> Death invaded earth and came face-to-face with heaven.
> Death relied on what was seen, and fell by what is unseen.
>
> O Death, where is your sting?
> O Grave, where is your victory?
> Christ has risen from the dead,
>> and become the firstborn of the dead.
> Glory and power to him forever and ever![3]

I called out, "Christ is risen!"

"He is risen indeed!" everyone responded.

We turned to find the Easter fire burning in the fire pit. The solar-powered twinkle lights strung above the sanctuary created a magical wonderland in the fading light. Sara taught us the Easter Troparion, a celebratory hymn from the Orthodox Church. "Christ is risen from the dead, trampling down death by death, and on those in the tombs bestowing life," we sang as we made our way around the altar, stomping our feet on the dusty ground, trampling down death by death. We shared communion together and then, after getting our bowls of soup and pieces of crusty bread, came back around the sanctuary and sat on blankets and camping chairs around the fire.

Soon Terese and Leia began bouncing up and down, singing, "Time for s'mores, time for s'mores, time for s'mores!" Willow unveiled the tower of marshmallows, graham crackers, and chocolate. Danny pulled out his guitar, and he and Ed began jamming. Then Danny moved to the keyboard, where his background as both a worship leader and musician who played gigs and on film sets was revealed. He played eclectic mash-ups of '90s evangelical worship songs intermixed with Beatles covers. Leia and Terese danced around the sanctuary area, their hands clasped together as they swung around and around. Asher, Nora, and I sat near the fire, roasting our marshmallows.

"Ooh, look at that one," I exclaimed, admiring Nora's perfectly-browned marshmallow, "just the way you've always liked to cook yours." Just then, Asher's burst out in flame, and we laughed.

"And that's just how I like to cook mine," he said.

I looked around at the people gathered. Peter had been pulled onto the dance floor with his granddaughter, Leia, and Willow and Doug were swaying together on the side. Danny had moved into other decades now, and most of us started singing along as Matt Redman's "The Heart of Worship" moved into "What the world needs now is love sweet love." I looked out on the quiet street, which was surprisingly peaceful for a Saturday evening, and thought about how much I loved this place.

If I needed to leave it so that my fiancé and I could be in the same location, it would not be easy. Sitting on the ground near that cedar stump, God's table where all are welcome, I felt so at home. These were my people; this was my church. Something new had been born and grown.

"You know," I heard Sara explaining to Terese, Willow, and Doug, "Easter is traditionally a time for baptisms."

"That's right," I chimed in, then half-jokingly called out, "Anyone want to get baptized tomorrow?"

A few minutes later, Peter approached me. "Actually, I do," he said. "I want to get baptized."

My face betrayed me as my jaw dropped open. "Aren't you already?"

Involved and dedicated Peter—I had assumed he had been baptized years ago, but no. Raised in a nominally religious family, and then married to a devout Catholic but not practicing himself, he had never taken the step.

"I never imagined I would find a band of like-minded, intrepid souls ready to worship with the earth beneath our feet, with our cultural differences, intellectual freedom, social justice . . . we are all imagining a new way of life expressing the abiding love modeled by Jesus," he mused, a thoughtful look in his eye. "This is my church," he said, looking right at me. "I would like to be baptized here."

"Okay," I replied, brushing aside fleeting thoughts of requiring classes and study, "I'll rework the liturgy for the morning."

Sara and I stayed up late that evening; I was adding a baptism service into our Easter liturgy and she was adjusting her sermon to integrate and point to the baptism. We went to bed tired but happy. After forty days of wandering through the wilderness of Lent, Palm Sunday, Maundy Thursday, Good Friday, and Holy Saturday, Easter was finally here.

*

"And very early on the first day of the week, when the sun had risen, they went to the tomb" (Mark 16:2). Although morning came too early for my body the next day, these words inspired us to meet for worship in the morning on Easter, the one Sunday of the year we didn't meet in the afternoon. I pulled a big batch of communion bread out of the oven, with a few dressed-up scones for our breakfast. "This is a good reason to stay at the pastor's house," Sara remarked as she ate the scone with her coffee.

When we arrived at the Garden Church, we saw we weren't the only women who were up early for Easter morning. Connie and Linda were already there, doing one of Connie's very favorite activities: re-costuming Dino for the occasion, changing out the palm branches and black shrouds for a white cape and angel wings. Pastel flowers replaced a crown of thorns. The wooden sign quoting Matthew 25:35, "For I was a stranger and you welcomed me," was left in its place in Dino's arms. We had made and hung the sign in January when airports across the country had been flooded with people calling for just immigration policies. Months later, the sign continued to proclaim the truth we wanted to live within those gates: welcome Jesus in the form of the stranger, in the form of each person we met.

"Happy Easter!" Connie called out as we made our way through the back gate.

"Christ has risen!" Linda shouted across the garden.

"He has risen indeed!" I replied.

The food tables were set up in time for the abundance of Easter breads that began flowing in from Annette's and Willow's cars. Over the past few years, our Easter service had been growing in popularity The egg hunt afterwards, in and amongst the garden beds, was a hit as well.

"We're like a 'regular' church," I chuckled. "Pastries and coffee and *worship on Sunday morning*!" We laughed at how absurd this norm felt for us.

Jedi was there, as he often was, but this time joined by his sister and parents, who usually refrained from coming so that Jedi could have a place that was all his own. They were joining us today for the special service.

As Linda played "Morning Has Broken," everyone found their seats in their Easter best—the garden-friendly version. By the time we had unpacked the tabernacle, sung the Easter classic "When Very Early in the Dawn," and Octavia read the Scripture, a good-sized crowd had gathered, full of regulars and a smattering of people I hadn't met before.

I invited Peter to come up to be baptized. A trio of mourning doves started singing from their perch on the wall of the building next to us. Peter came forward, along with his wife, Linda, and their daughter Sarah, her husband, Ed, and granddaughter Leia. We clustered together at the front of the sanctuary area. I opened my mouth to begin the baptism readings, when I was interrupted.

"Wait, wait," Annette's voice called from across the sanctuary. "He needs a godmother. I will be his godmother."

I was taken aback. In my pastoral experience, godparent arrangements are usually made in advance. Generally a good friend or sibling of the parent takes on the role of supporting the person being baptized (or supporting the parents, if an infant is being baptized). But here was Annette, in her late sixties, using her cane to navigate the dirt floor, making her way up to be godmother to sixty-five-year-old Peter.

"Umm . . ." I said, fumbling over my words as I took in the scene, "Peter, would you like a godmother? Would you like Annette to be your godmother?"

"I'd be honored," was Peter's reply.

The water dripped from my fingers as I made the sign of the cross on Peter's wrinkled forehead. I remembered the first baptism we had had around this table: his granddaughter, Leia, who was now standing tall on her own and helping Linda hold the baptismal candle. Here we were, a church.

Baptism complete, Sara got up to preach, and I smiled with gratitude. She was one of the few people I would offer my pulpit to on a holiday like this, but I did it gladly—insisting, really. "You miss preaching," I had said to her a few weeks prior. "And the congregation hears me plenty." The truth was that *I* needed to hear her sermon.

"What do they need to hear?" Sara had asked me.

"I think they need to have reflected back to them who they are as a church, and that they are a church," I responded. "They need to hear someone other than me witnessing and telling them that they are God's church, not Reverend Anna's church, and that the church persists throughout time."

Sara's sermon did that and more as she named the story of Easter morning within the story of Holy Week, the story of the Garden Church, and the story of God and the church throughout generations. As she told of Jesus revealing himself to his disciples on the road to Emmaus, she pointed to how Jesus reveals himself to us as we make church together. "What happened on the road to Emmaus—and what I've seen during this Holy Week with you at the Garden Church—offer some hints about how to meet and joyfully know the resurrected Lord," she said.[4]

Sara outlined ways of meeting and knowing the resurrected Christ. "One: Walk together, talk together, work
together," she said. "You're on your way somewhere through
the ordinary, screwed-up streets of your own town, having
a bad day, or maybe just busy, but you meet a friend, and
walk alongside them, and then you both meet a stranger who
joins you, and then you all keep going past the bus stops and
pawnshops, and stop to pick up something for dinner, and
offer to carry stuff for each other, and holiness breaks in.
That's what happened in Emmaus, it's what happened this
week in San Pedro, and it's what still happens every time we
make church together."

As Sara preached, I noticed a man hovering outside the
gates. I waved at him, but he didn't come in. He walked a
little further down the fence and looked through. I leaned over
to Connie and whispered, "Would you go do your friendly,
welcoming thing?"

Connie pushed back her big straw hat and walked over to
the man. She listened to him tenderly and led him to the food
tables to get him a cup of coffee. He hurriedly drank it, then
asked for another. And another. Connie refilled it a third time,
but when he asked for a fourth cup her mothering instinct
overtook her hospitality and she filled it instead with water.

"Two: Worship together," Sara continued. "Because Jesus
appears whenever believers, doubters, and seekers gather, and
scatter, and run away and come back together again to share
their experiences, and shine the light of Scripture on them.
Because when we listen deeply to the songs and stories of our
ancestors, and discover new meanings through sharing our
own stories of where we saw God, Jesus will make himself
known. That's what happened on the road to Emmaus, and

it's what happened this week in San Pedro, and it's what still happens every time we make church together.

"Three: Eat together. We continue in the breaking of bread, because Jesus longs to eat with his friends. So haul yourself to the table when you're sad and lost; when you don't know or don't trust the people around you, when you're afraid Jesus is dead and you'll never find him again. And then—make even the smallest gesture of friendship, of hospitality, of love toward a stranger, and Jesus will show up. That's what happened in Emmaus, and it's what happened this week in San Pedro, and it's what still happens every time we make church together."

Just as Sara began to talk about eating together, Connie pulled a large cream brioche and glazed donut from the table for the man, then offered him a large woven Easter hat to shade him from the hot morning sun.

Sara continued to preach, not knowing that her teaching was being enacted directly behind her. "We make church," she said, "but really, Christ Jesus is making church, as we work and worship and eat together, and so become his body. In bread and wine, in water and in dirt, in marshmallows over a new fire, we become his resurrected, *living* body.

"Remember the good news: Christ is risen, in San Pedro just as on the road to Emmaus. Christ is risen, and has come today to seal our brother Peter, and each one of us, as his own forever. Christ is risen, and is here with us, even to the end of ages."

As Sara concluded her sermon, the man thanked Connie and walked out of the gates, adorned with his new Easter bonnet and the joy of resurrection.

-12-
TREE OF LIFE

After Holy Week, time seemed to speed up. David and I were to be married in May, and we were weighing and wondering what was next for our shared geography. At church, events zoomed by faster than I could wrap my head around. We held our second Earth Day expo and interfaith service and celebrated the church's third birthday. During our first-ever membership Sunday, twenty-one people officially joined the church. I felt these as blessings; I also felt like I was running a marathon.

I left for two weeks at the end of May for our wedding in Colorado and a little honeymoon after. As I left, I could sense the tension of people wondering, "What is next? Is Reverend Anna going to leave us?"

"David and I will be here for the summer. I have signed a contract through the end of the year, and we'll see after that," I reminded them, though my uncertainty about the future could not be masked. Being away for two weeks was unsettling in itself, but I knew the church was in good hands; Revs. Asher and Amanda would fill in for me on the Sundays, and Bree would keep everything running.

When David and I returned to LA as a married couple, we settled into my small apartment and quickly fell into a lovely rhythm of work, rest, and play. It was suddenly difficult to work until all hours of the night; after so many years living solo, I now had a sweet husband to come home to and adventure with. He made lunch in the middle of busy work days and happily engaged in church events. In the preceding summer and during subsequent visits, David had become a beloved member of the community, and people were glad to now have him there every week.

The congregation, wanting to celebrate our marriage, threw us a blessing service.

We got gussied up in our wedding garb. I was happy to have an excuse to wear my wedding dress again and see David in his tuxedo. Connie had hunted down a real-life red carpet for us to walk on. Garden Church flower girls awaited us—Farmer Lara's daughter Sabine, plus Terese, Leia, and Angie, a little girl who had been coming to church for the past few weeks.

The garden had been transformed. Extra shade shelters were borrowed and chairs arranged underneath them. Sarah and Ed generously loaned the white satin covers from their wedding to beautify our folding chairs. There were flowers everywhere. My friend Michael, the music director at Wayfarers Chapel, had arranged a string quartet to play for us as a wedding gift.

We made our way up the carpet, looking joyfully at each face as we walked in, and sat at the front of the sanctuary. We had asked Revs. Asher and Amanda to officiate the service, and they had invited others of our clergy friends in the area to participate as well. To begin the service, each of them took an object out of the tabernacle and talked about it in their own way.

Rev. Dave, a friend from Wayfarers Chapel who had supported the Garden Church since the very beginning, spoke about the final object, the tree of life icon. Dave reminded us where we find this tree—at the very end of the book of Revelation, where the vision of the heavenly city, the New Jerusalem, is given. As he held it up and I looked around, I could see and feel the power of lifting that icon up every week over the years; when these people saw that icon, it was a reminder of the vision we were striving to be part of. Our little plot of land in the middle of the city was ours to cultivate into being a little bit more like the heavenly city, here on earth.

Linda began playing the bars of the opening hymn on the piano, and we sang one of David's and my favorites, "For everyone born, a place at the table."[1] The song speaks of room for all at God's feasting table. I sang, as I looked out at the congregation gathered around us.

I listened as David's deep bass sang of the need for clean water and bread for all people.

I watched Farmer Lara, not in her usual jeans and a button-down shirt, but in a floral sundress and even makeup, sitting with her kids, beaming at us. Her son sat next to Jedi. The two of them, though a few years apart, regularly spent time talking about Star Wars and Minecraft while working in the garden. Next to them was Katie in her tattered shorts. A kindergarten teacher and a port official sat next to Hilton, whose eye, I noticed, was black. His face was a bit bloody too.

I got teary as we sang of God's shelter for and delight in all creation, and I caught my husband's eye. I leaned over to him and whispered in his ear, "Thank you for not only being supportive of my ministry, but also for *getting* that this is the kingdom of God."

Asher gave a beautiful sermon and Nora sang the song she had written for our engagement gift. David and I, overflowing with love, looked into each other's eyes and back to our dear sister. Our clergy friends laid their hands on us, praying and blessing us as the passing of the peace went along. When it came time for communion, I watched Asher, Amanda, Connie, and Peter serve everyone, including people along the edges.

After communion and a big wedding feast and cake, I heard another side to the day—all the other things that had made it church. Albert, who had been routinely interrupting the sermon and liturgy with his own reflections and ideas for the last month or so, had come in during the beginning of the service. Connie, who was at the gate welcoming people, said to him, "Today is going to be about listening, just listening; there is not going to be a time for you to speak today."

Albert thought hard about it for a moment, then said, "Okay, I'll come back at five for dinner then." When he returned, he very respectfully shook both David's and my hand, wishing us congratulations and blessings.

The core church leaders kept the big upset from me until cleanup time. They may have waited even longer if I hadn't suspected and asked Willow what was up. Our little heaven here on earth had not been very peaceful that day after all.

While they were scrambling to finish setting up before the service, Dan and Hilton had come in, bringing an altercation that had been brewing since the night before at the bar. It quickly escalated into a physical fight—the first we'd dealt with within our gates. The police had been summoned, and Dan had been taken away. I now understood the shaken look on Bree's face when she had first met us at the gate, and Hilton's black eye and bloodied cheek.

In that moment, I turned from bride to pastor and moved into incident reporting forms, policy reinforcement, and leading a debrief, all while standing on the bench of the picnic table, trying to keep my white dress out of the dust.

I didn't sleep much that night, thinking about it all. I was torn between celebration in community and disappointment about the violent incident within our gates.

The thing about the heavenly city is that it is an ideal. We look towards it, work for it, yearn for it. We may catch glimpses of it. But we are not there yet. We live firmly rooted in this broken and struggling world, where people hit each other instead of talking towards reconciliation, and where addiction, poverty, and pain are always present. As we explored this way of being church, we were constantly being challenged to hold the both/and, the now-and-not-yet, the world we lived in and the world we believed God was also yearning to bring into being. We raised our tree of life icon to remember its place in the heavenly city and our commitment to doing our part to bring more justice and peace and healing and transformation to our city.

Lifting that icon up each week that summer also reminded me that this work was God's, not only mine. And God's work was shared with others—others were feeling the call to lead this church together. When the last no from David's job applications in the Los Angeles area came through in the end of June, we made the hard decision that I would leave the Garden Church at the end of the year and we would make a home in upstate New York where he had a job.

On one hand, it all felt so clear. I had been called to plant this church, to begin it, and now I was being called to the next season of my life and ministry. The church was strong and could go on without me. On the other, I felt a knot in the pit of my stomach whenever I thought about telling the board, the congregation, the more than two hundred donors from across the country who had been supporting the effort, and the denominational leaders who had given so much. I was afraid I would be disappointing them all by not staying and continuing to pastor the church. Beyond my mixed-up feelings of worry and guilt, I was sad. David was too. We loved these people and this church.

When these feelings grew too strong, I went into problem-solving and planning mode. I decided that if I was going to break this news and make this hard transition, I would do so with as much forethought and strategy as I could muster. While people might have strong reservations about me leaving, they would know what the plan was—and that they would be taken care of no matter what.

With much prayer and many conversations with the people closest to the church, by the time I arrived at the pivotal board meeting at the end of June, we had a general plan sketched out.

The board sat around the table in the upstairs room at the British Pub on 7th Street, and Jana chaired the meeting with her usual wisdom and efficiency. "We have a lot of important things to decide on tonight," she said after our opening prayer, "so we're going to start out with putting things on the table.

Let's start by naming our hopes and our fears." The anticipation in the room was palpable, along with some relief that we were actually going to *talk* about the anxieties, questions, and concerns around the table.

"I hope that we can continue as a church without Reverend Anna. I'm afraid we won't be able to," summed up most everyone's comments.

I felt the weight of it all in my chest. It was time to agree on a way forward.

We discussed the plan I had developed in the past few weeks in my many conversations and prayers. The church would remain under my leadership until September, when we would enter into a four-month transition time. I would work half-time, allowing me to spend time with David in New York, and a pastoral transition team would guide the church through the fall: Rev. Jonathan, who had moved back to the area to live with his partner, Carl, after going into semiretirement; Rev. Asher, who had continued to get involved in his extra time each week; and Rev. Amanda, whose service on the board and general involvement had grown. These incredible ministers had already been involved with the Garden Church, and were known, loved, and trusted by the congregation. At the end of December, after these four months of transition, I would leave. The transition team would continue to lead until, at some point in the following year, the church board would hire a new pastor or pastors.

People had good questions and adjustments to this plan, but all in all, there was a big sigh of relief.

"So you're not leaving us *right now*," TeaJ said.

"And we love and trust Amanda and Jonathan and Asher," Peter chimed in.

Jana reminded us that we were a church that had always been mindful of creative adjustment and change. People come and go, but the mission of an organization can persist.

By the end of the board meeting, there was a unanimous vote to move forward with the transition plan.

When we came to closing thoughts at the meeting, the room was not just peaceful, but a bit excited about what God was doing and what could come next. "I've brought communion. Anyone want some?" I asked with a smile. As I spoke those familiar words around the table, I thought back to the early board meetings in my living room, before we had a plot of land or even a congregation. We'd sit around my large thrift store coffee table and brainstorm, making fundraising plans, arguing, and dreaming. At the end of those retreats, we would always have communion around the table.

"Someday you'll have a congregation and a local group of people to create your board," Jane, our first board chair, had said back at the beginning of the church. I believed her, but only kind of. That, or we'll close before we even start, and I'll be searching for a job, I had thought.

Four years later, here I was, sitting around a table with a local board and an established church. So many new people had caught the vision and gotten involved. "Amanda, beloved child of God, the bread of life, given for you. TeaJ, beloved child of God, the bread of life, given for you." I made my way around the table and ended with Jana, my dear friend and our board chair who had had my back, behind the scenes, through the whole process. "Jana, beloved child of God." My voice wavered as the tears would not be stopped. "The bread of life, given for you." After we'd all eaten, I held up the tree of life icon again and said, "We keep coming back to it, we keep gathering around it. You will keep being church, friends. Every time you unpack this basket."

Over the next days I individually emailed longtime supporters, family, and friends about the decision before it went out publicly. I was relieved and grateful for the supportive and understanding responses. People could see and be excited about the future for the Garden Church with new leadership in place.

The one response that I read over and over again, letting the words sink in, was from Grandma Gladish, my cherished ninety-one-year-old last living grandparent. She had supported the Garden Church from before it began with her prayers and belief in my and God's ability to lead it. "Dear Anna," she wrote,

> Blessings on the next step in your lives—a commitment that far exceeds any organization in this world.
>
> Actually, no questions about your decisions and no great surprise! You have been working toward a useful and orderly transition for quite some time, just as you worked toward the establishment of the Garden Church, which is certainly in the Lord's hands. Time for the next phase of life, and all the engaging things that will bring. What you have done will be in your heart and mind as others carry on.
>
> Thanks for including me. I appreciate your thoughtful mind and letter.
>
> Love and love to you both,
>
> Grandma

As the summer progressed, the "You're leaving?" conversation found a peaceful place. I savored my final months as the pastor at this messy and beautiful congregation, soaking up the time with new appreciation. I felt lighter, somehow, and more willing to laugh and appreciate when unexpected things happened.

In the fall I moved my living essentials into Nora's apartment and packed the rest into a moving truck. For the next months, I would rotate my time between upstate New York and San Pedro. When I returned to San Pedro after my first two weeks away, the transition team was bubbling over with questions and stories. We sat around a table in the Methodist church, where we had set up an office for the Garden Church after I moved out of my apartment. Connie and Linda joined us for the start of the meeting.

"You know Betty?" Linda asked, looking at me expectantly.

"Of course," I replied, picturing the stocky woman with blonde hair who had become a regular over the summer. She would carefully park her shopping cart beside the prayer garden and near the gate before coming to dinner. She never said much at dinner, and struggled to answer people's friendly questions, but had started coming earlier and earlier. She had even accepted a hug from me when I'd given her communion.

"Well," Linda continued, "Betty came at the beginning of worship this week. And I made an announcement encouraging that we collect and bring in any leaves we might find this fall for our compost. After worship, Betty asked for a plastic bag so she could collect leaves at the park and bring them to compost!"

Connie beamed as Linda told the story, then said, "Who knows what will happen, but she was so sincere and it was the most words she's ever said to me, and she had the intention and desire to contribute to the community."

On Sunday, I continued a worship series I'd begun a few weeks earlier about the objects in our church in a basket. I wanted to remind them, before I left, of who they were—and their history and principles as a church.

I talked about our first service in the park on the San Pedro cliffs, back before we built a home on 6th Street. I had filled a basket with the things we needed for that very first worship time—the Bible, the candleholder, the bread, the stainless steel water bottles that held water and juice, the cups, and the tree of life icon. These items—candles, Bibles, water, and bread—shaped us as a church. When we took them from the basket each week, we were reminded of how we were called to love God and love our neighbor.

On another Sunday, I preached about bread, about feeding and being fed. We discussed the idea that while everyone is hungry for something, everyone has something to offer as well, as we had seen so beautifully with the thousands of people who had come through our gates. So many of our community members spent much of their time waiting in lines to *ask* for things: food, shelter, jobs, healthcare, assistance. They were another case, another file, another person *needing* something. And yet, when they came in through the gates of the Garden Church, they could be *needed* as well as having need. We needed Jarrett to help water and Danny to play his guitar. We needed Randy to help turn the compost and Brad to help build garden beds.

During the reflection time after the sermon, Linda said, "I sometimes wonder whether our message of creating community in order to create peace and justice is perceived by the visitors to our garden. Then my doubts are dispelled by a spontaneous comment someone makes." She spoke about working with a woman at Friday's gardening time. The woman was fulfilling a court order for volunteer hours, and she and Linda spent the time hauling compost. "Together we pulled a heavy cart full of vegetable peelings and coffee grounds we had collected from a local restaurant, taking them to our compost bins," Linda said. "We passed people coming in and out of the stores, restaurants, and tattoo parlors on 6th Street, when she said, 'The thing about the Garden Church is that, of all these places on 6th Street, the Garden Church has heart.'"

I looked at Linda's wise eyes and thought about how her experience of the Garden Church had shifted over the months and years. She'd been skeptical at first, having spent her life dedicated to churches that took place in brick and mortar buildings. But as her granddaughter and daughter, and then her son-in-law and husband began attending, she began to wonder. The challenge to reimagine church, and how that had unfolded in the garden, had cracked the more rigid religious customs she had practiced for years, and shed a new light on practices and definitions she had taken for granted. She had once told me that at the Garden Church "it felt like my inner flowers were opening up to the light. It dawned on me that if we are the living stones of the church, we don't need bricks!"

People who came into the garden often remarked on its beauty, saying that getting their hands in the dirt made them feel renewed and reconnected. But it was more than just a community garden, it was truly a sanctuary, a church, a dedicated sacred space where people's spirits were fed as we kept showing up and being needed as we made church together.

I was lucky enough to be at church when Betty came in while we were passing the peace, her shopping cart loaded down a bit more than usual with the three big trash bags that Linda had given her—stuffed full of dried leaves for the compost. As Betty crossed over the threshold of our gates, from the reality of the brokenness of her city to this little urban garden trying to be a little bit more like heaven here on earth, she had a big smile on her face.

The Bible begins in the garden of Eden, with the tree of life at its center. It is an idyllic place where people walk with God in innocence, connection, and intimacy with the sacred. At the end of the Bible, we see the heavenly city, New Jerusalem. At its center is the tree we saw in the garden of Eden. The tree is in the middle again, calling people to it, but this time via twelve different gates, to a place where God is present and drawing us together.

Leading up to the planting of the Garden Church, I had studied and worked with church dynamics, asking questions such as: What leads to belonging? What keeps us apart? How do space and place and culture define our sense of self and community?

So often our experience of belonging in community is defined by crossing over a barrier. If you believe a certain way, you can cross over the fence. Maybe you need to look a certain way or dress a certain way. Maybe your relationships and family have to work within certain definitions. Maybe you have to be okay and have it together in order to belong.

These are simple, common dynamics. One of the easiest ways to ensure that we belong to the in-crowd is to make sure we all know who's *not* in it. We build these fences and we may begin to think we are safe, even superior, while we are within them. We reinforce our belonging by making sure we're all clear on who is *out*. When we're feeling vulnerable about our own belonging, our own wholeness, our own belovedness, we form a bond with our in-crowd based on our exclusion of others. But our fences, carefully constructed and guarded, do not form the boundaries of the kingdom of God. These fences do not shelter the beloved community. These fences do not embody the work of God's incarnate love.

Instead, God calls us to the table, where all are welcome to feed and be fed. The table draws us together; it is a magnet pulling us into beloved community rather than a fence that we have to cross over. You belong by the very fact that you are moving toward the center. As we are drawn together, we notice that the people on either side of us are not necessarily like us. Gathering around God's table, we soon find that we are interacting with people we would not have otherwise. In discovering that all kinds of people belong to God, we in turn learn that we belong to all kinds of people.

This felt true as we wove together various branches of the Christian family tree in our little garden. This tree has split, and split, and split again over the decades and centuries. And in that variety has grown as different branches bear unique fruits as people express their beliefs in different ways and add to the beauty and diversity of the church. We saw this especially in the clergy who ministered within our gates. Rev. Amanda, with her sharp brain and her Presbyterian propensity towards order and structure, kept things running and organized, and provided a space for others to give their gifts. Rev. Jonathan, deeply steeped in the Swedenborgian worldview of finding good in many religious paths, practiced regularly at a Buddhist sangha and brought teachings of acceptance and understanding to our team and community. Rev. Asher brought a rich love for the tradition of the liturgy. His faith had roots in the Lutheran family tree, specifically the House for All Sinners and Saints in Denver, whose founding pastor Nadia Bolz-Weber had built the church while holding the principle "Faith must be deeply rooted in tradition in order to innovate with integrity." Our neighbor down the street, Pastor Lisa, is a third-generation Methodist pastor, who took seriously words often attributed to church founder John Wesley: "Do all the good you can, by all the means you can, in all the ways you can, in all the places you can, at all the times you can, to all the people you can." She and I talked often about how our work to pastor churches in downtown San Pedro and the community was work that our grandparents and great-grandparents would have been proud of.

Coming together in this community had loosened our grips on some ideas. Amanda let go of us not all seeing the Trinity in exactly the same way. Connie nuanced her view on the bread being Christ's literal body. Peter was loosening his skepticism about Jesus in the first place. We didn't abandon our traditions, but as we focused on breaking bread and sharing in the work of the community, it seemed that the things that divided us diminished, and the things that brought us together increased. I found myself reflecting on a well-worn passage in Emanuel Swedenborg's works: "...if we considered love for the Lord and charity for our neighbor the chief concern of faith. If we did . . . one church would come out of all the different churches, and all disagreement due to doctrine alone would vanish. Even the hatred of one denomination for another would melt away in a moment, and the Lord's kingdom would come on earth."[2]

When we saw glimpses of this vision, it reminded us why it is important that people come together and make church together. We got our hands dirty and saw how God was calling us to love one another in tangible, physical ways. Collectively, we were capable of more love than any of us could enact on our own.

When we gathered at the table, we remembered that we belonged to God and we belonged to each other. Not because of what we had in common, but because of who we were in common: children of God.

Our third annual harvest celebration came together through miracles, hard work, and sheer willpower. The extra lights were strung, the stage was constructed, long tables with auction items were set, and food—harvested from the garden and prepared by a new catering company from the Beacon House Men's Recovery Home—was being laid out on the tables. "How are we doing, Peter?" I asked as he scurried around, getting the big screen for the projector attached to the brick wall.

"It's happening!" he said with a smile. "We've got quite a team."

I looked around at the variety of people who were already there. Jedi with his mom and sister putting the finishing touches on the auction baskets. Katie, Octavia, and a friend putting out vases of flowers. Connie came in with a huge basket filled with little jars of herbs that she had harvested and dried from the garden over the past months and began arranging them on the farm stand. Rev. Jonathan and his partner, Carl, figured out how to work the credit card swiper on their phones and set up the welcome table at the front gate. We had told the whole community that because it was a fundraiser, there was a ticket price, but anyone who wanted to come and volunteer could get a free ticket. A whole handful of our unhoused neighbors came early for set-up and returned in the evening for the celebration.

A jazz trio played as folks talked and ate hors d'oeuvres. The president of the chamber of commerce, major patrons in the community, people from Wayfarers Chapel, local clergy, and a full turnout from our congregation all mingled together. After the chamber president and I gave a welcome, I gave our cultivator of the year award to our beloved Farmer Lara, who had recently moved on to pursue her dream of having a farm of her own. She was growing food in a once-empty lot about ten blocks from us. I shared about how we had first met at her little farm table at the Corner Store when I moved to San Pedro, and about all the dreaming and scheming she and her husband, Scott, and I had done at her kitchen table. I thanked her for the hundreds of hours she had given to our community, naming how beloved she was by many for sharing her garden wisdom, kind hugs, and always some new and creative vegetables that we'd never seen before. Lara was expanding a vision we had all shared around their kitchen table—what if all the empty land in San Pedro was growing food?

Lara's response brought a smile to my face as she reflected on her part in growing this vision. "Before the Garden Church," she said, "I was always passionate about growing food in any place I lived. I also knew from some of those experiences that interacting with nature and growing food is good for people, regardless of their age and background. But knowing it in my mind, and actually experiencing it with thousands of people over the course of two years, did more than solidify that knowledge—it amplified it."

I thought of Lara's steady presence and the way she had welcomed and treated each person who came through our gates with dignity and care.

"There are so many ways of interacting in the garden, and the path to transformation can be so simple, yet so different for everyone," she continued. "Whether it's an educational experience, or a religious experience, or simply taking a breath during a horrible day, working with food and nature in an urban sanctuary has the power to transform people for the better."

I hugged Lara as she left the stage. "We did it," she said. "I am so impressed that we were able to create such a dynamic sanctuary and space that is still thriving today. I walk in here now and still see some of the things that I planted so long ago, still producing and growing, and how the people there are just enjoying it. It feels good."

After showing the crowd a reminder of where we had come from—a photo of the empty lot—we cast a vision of what was to come next. Peter shared about the plan for vertical garden beds and raising the edges of existing beds to grow plants that needed deeper roots. We moved into a time of giving and a silent auction, and I smiled gently as I watched people's generosity soar. Within minutes we had raised more than our goal, as everyone pitched in what they could. Yet again we had enough. Enough, and some to share.

This was how the whole church had been supported in the first place: seminary students pledging ten dollars a month, a few people giving large chunks of start-up funding, and the denomination and many others giving steadily and generously along the way. Tears came to my eyes as I thought of all the people who had made this dream possible with their prayers, their giving, and their participation. Yes, at times I had felt it to be a solo effort, but this was never actually the case. People across the globe, many of whom had never even been able to visit in person, had brought this vision into being with me, and their hearts were woven into the fabric of this church.

The jazz trio started playing again, and I stood by the stage to watch for a while. Amanda's mother and some of her friends from their church sat at a table chatting with Katie and her boyfriend, Tom, while Katie's dog, Diana, quietly sat under the table. Jedi was presiding over the farm stand and telling people about the kale and Swiss chard and dried herbs. Carl had gotten a break from the front table and was sitting on a hay bale, deep in conversation with a woman who had come, even though large crowds made her nervous, wearing her best and cleanest clothing for the evening—a pair of matching floral flannel pajamas. I watched as Jarrett approached a server who was passing out bruschetta. "Can I have one?" he asked.

The server looked skeptically at Jarrett's tattered vest and camo shorts. "Um, I'll have to ask my supervisor," he said.

Jarrett stood up tall and said, "Hey now, I water this garden! I can eat what we grew here." The server handed him an appetizer as I stepped over to reinforce that Jarrett was indeed an invited guest and part of the team.

All kinds of people coming together around God's table to feed and be fed, I thought. Here is the dream.

I recalled how, in college, one of my mentors had pulled me aside at the church he had planted in Tucson. We were standing in the sanctuary at Sunrise Chapel and looking out the long picture windows that framed the mountains around Tucson and highlighted the giant saguaro cacti growing in the gardens behind the altar. He had put his long arm around my shoulder.

"See this?" he said in his low, wise voice. "You're standing in my vision."

His words echoed back to me as I stood there, looking around our garden sanctuary. "See this?" I prayed quietly. "I'm standing in our vision, God. I'm standing in our vision."

When I returned the next month, I was met by a long list of problems and questions at our staff meeting. Some were easily answered and some were more complicated. I felt in myself the tension between wanting to just jump into problem-solving mode and the more important need to support this group in rising into leadership together. I also felt the weight of passing on the church's core values and institutional memory.

At the last leadership table meeting I attended, Jana and I led a process of telling our origin story as a church, starting from the very beginning. I took a stack of small cardboard boxes and labeled them for each season, starting back in 2013 and up to fall 2017. I wrote the key events that had happened in each season at the Garden Church on the appropriate box.

With all four heaters fired up and the lights twinkling over-head, we placed the boxes chronologically around the sanctuary area and invited people to find the box where they had entered the story, put their name on the box, and add things to the story after they entered it. After everyone had added their anecdotes, I began narrating the story and inviting others to join in. When we would get to someone's name, I'd invite them to tell about how they first encountered the Garden Church, their early impressions, and why they stayed.

Rev. Jonathan talked about how he first encountered the Garden Church even earlier, back in 2011 when he was on my ordination committee and I first started talking about the church I wanted to plant.

Rev. Amanda shared about how we met for coffee down the street the first fall I was there. She was a year into a church plant; I was just beginning. We had immediately bonded.

Nancy shared her memory of the very beginning. "Remember the first gathering we had? You asked everyone there what gifts they had that they wanted to offer the project, and I said networking." I remembered this with a smile; Nancy had taken that seriously and had connected us with many of the people who had become integral to the church.

"Nancy, think about it," I continued. "You and I are the only people from that informational gathering who are around this circle tonight. People come and go, but the church remains."

Connie remembered first meeting me briefly soon after I'd moved to town, but not getting involved until over a year later. Her life had been changed for the better, she said.

Peter remembered coming in when we were open for a First Thursday art walk and seeing the lights and the music and thinking, "I've always dreamed this place could be something like this—but this is even better."

Linda recounted being skeptical of the whole thing at first, but seeing that her daughter and granddaughter were so engaged that she kept coming back and fell in love.

Jedi recounted in his deepening sixteen-year-old voice that this was the place he felt like he belonged the past three years, and added, "We forgot a major milestone—summer

2016—our first artichoke! Do you know how long it took to grow that and how long we waited for it?"

Nora wasn't sure when she'd first entered the picture; being my sister, she'd been hearing about my dreams since before they were fully formed. She put her name on the box labeled "Spring 2015," which was when she had moved across the country and became involved with the Garden Church in earnest. She expressed that since coming here from a conservative religious tradition, her view of God and religion had grown. She was shown her lack of awareness of her privilege, and racial, economic, and heteronormative background and views. "Before moving to LA, I didn't count how many people of color were in the room or have any awareness of being queer-friendly," she said. "I had no empathy for those who feel alone in a full room. I am still privileged, but in the past I didn't notice that. Now I try to notice."

Willow remembered when she and Terese first came in, having just moved to town. "We are used to moving regularly, and finding community is tough," she recounted. "Finding the Garden Church jump-started it this time. It was a place where Terese could thrive and be involved."

Amanda recalled how her then six-year-old son had first come to the Garden Church and said, "Mama! There's no roof! It's a church with no roof! It is so special, I don't know *any* other churches that don't have roofs!"

Jana brought it full circle; she articulated the arc of our story, stressing the importance of the church being beyond the space or specifics, but *who we are together*. She spoke to our commitment to faith over fear, to trusting God in the process. We looked at the stack of empty boxes I had placed at the end of the circle.

"You have a good future ahead of you," I said, willing it into my words. "This expression of church is part of the stories of faith throughout history, and regardless of how long it shows up in this particular form, it's making its contribution to the community and to the church as a whole."

We ended with a principle that was part of the church's original DNA: "What you celebrate grows." There are certainly times and places for good critique, yet we sought the spiritual practice of gratitude and celebration at the Garden Church. I reminded the leadership table that it was their job to remember to notice and celebrate too.

To conclude the meeting, everyone shared something that they had noticed at church in the past week that they wanted to celebrate. Amanda noticed the dedicated volunteers whom she saw day after day at the church. Peter noticed the incoming volunteers who were getting involved. Linda noticed the new baby carrots and the mustard greens ready to pick. Jedi noticed how the community was a safe place to be himself. Nora noticed the music, and how people had brought their musician friends so there were new faces at the jam session before worship on Sunday. Asher noticed the vibrancy of everything, from the green beans to the people. While my departure and the transition brought sadness, and while the church faced ongoing worries about money and stability and leadership, those fears and feelings were part of the story, but not the whole story. The deeper truth was that through grief and celebration, anxiety and hope, they could keep being church together.

-13-

CHURCH IN A BASKET

I landed at LAX in December, the familiar view of neighborhood after neighborhood stretching out below us as the plane descended. Even in its familiarity, the view now had a bittersweet tang: it was the last time I'd be making this cross-country commute to my job as pastor of the Garden Church.

Nora picked me up at the airport and drove me back to her apartment. I knew the first thing I had to do was to go see a member of the congregation who was sick. Karen had requested that I visit and bring communion to both her and her sister.

Karen was one of our founding members and had been with us through so much. The first day we opened the gates, it was Karen who had brought a cooler full of ice that she'd carefully frozen throughout the week, and she rolled that cooler over every Friday and every Sunday until her body wasn't able anymore.

Even when she couldn't come in person, Karen kept in touch. She entered the email addresses from the sign-up sheets into our database and insisted that I send her the prayer requests every week so she could pray for those suffering. I know she did it. She said her heart always remained with us.

Over the past few months, I'd offered to go visit, but she always insisted that she would get back to church. Finally she asked if I would come and see her, and bring communion.

Her sister met me in the parking lot of the condo complex where I approached with the tabernacle basket in hand. I gave her a hug, having met her a few times over the years.

"How are you doing?" I asked. Her face showed something deeper than simple tiredness.

"She's stopped taking all medications." I slowed to a stop and put my hand on her arm. "She's done. She's barely eating or drinking now."

"Has hospice come in?" I asked.

"Yes, they have. She has the bed and morphine and they check in. But they can't do much. She doesn't want to prolong it at this point."

I took a deep breath. Okay, I thought, this is a different kind of visit.

Inside, in the midst of a full little living room, I saw the back of a hospital bed.

"Hello, my dear," I gently called out. Karen answered in a weak voice. I set down the tabernacle and leaned over to hug her. "You are so beautiful!" I blurted out. Even in her obvious pain and weakened state, Karen was glowing; her white hair was combed back from her face, and she had a radiant smile.

I sat down by the bed. First Karen told me about her body, how she'd stopped taking the meds and was not eating or drinking much. Then I asked, "How's your spirit?"

"Ooh," she said, "my spirit is ready to go. I feel like I'm in both worlds right now."

"Cool! What are you seeing over there?" I asked.

"Oh, it's wonderful!" she exclaimed in a hoarse voice. "I'm picking out what neighborhood I want to live in. I think I'm going to pick the one where my job would be to scoop up little children who are just arriving and take care of them until they found their permanent home. I love scooping up little children and loving them."

I felt my throat tightening with tears. Over and over, I'd seen this to be true of Karen.

We talked of the Garden Church and Wayfarers Chapel and how involved she was early on. We talked of her daughter and son-in-law. We talked about her journey with illness and everything along the way.

I could see she was starting to get tired. "Should we have worship?" I suggested.

"Oh, yes, please!" she quietly replied.

I moved the TV tray over, pulled out a cloth from the basket, and spread it over the tray. And then, in the rhythm that had become so natural, yet in a setting that was so different, I pulled out the Bible and said the familiar words, "'In the beginning was the Word, and the Word was with God and the Word was God, and God came and pitched her tent among us, God came and set up his tabernacle among us.' And so, when we gather for worship in the spirit of the Garden Church, wherever we are, we remember that God is everywhere and moving in all things, and that God is right here, with us and amongst us. And so we unpack our tabernacle, our church in a basket, taking out these things that remind us of God's presence with us."

Karen's eyes followed my hands as I opened Bible. "The stories of God and the stories of humanity."

I lit the candle as I said, "The light, the light of Christ, the light that shines in the darkness and is not overcome and the light that we see when we look across the circle into each other's eyes and see the spark of the divine in all people." The sisters looked into each other's eyes, with the look of people who have been through a lot together.

I poured water into the stainless steel bowl and said, "The water, the water of life, the water that renews."

As I pulled items from the basket, I saw Karen nodding and even mouthing along with some of it as if she were seeing in each object an old friend. We got to the tree of life, and I reminded her that she had been part of cultivating those healing leaves, how more peace and justice and reconciliation and hope had been realized thanks to her faithful presence. She caressed the icon with her dry and delicate hands and nodded. "That place is a little bit of heaven here," she said, "a little bit of heaven."

I picked up the Bible and asked, "What's a favorite passage of yours?"

"Oh, Psalm 118, not 119. So many people like that one and it's so long, but I love Psalm 118." I started to read it. "Oh, please, won't you sing it?" Karen interjected. I couldn't get through all the lines without my voice cracking.

It was time to share the bread and cup. I chanted the communion prayers, taking the bread that had been blessed yesterday in community, and repeating the words that she and I both knew so well.

When I got to "Dear ones, this is God's table and all are welcome here, all you need to be to eat here is hungry," Karen said the words along with me, and with a sweet smile on her face.

"I'm hungry," she said. I took the smallest piece of bread, looked her in the eye, and said, "Karen, beloved child of God, the bread of life," and handed it to her. She carefully nibbled a quarter of it.

"This is more food than I've had in a while," she said.

She carefully chewed and then asked for the cup. I served her sister, and then turned to Karen and she served me.

We prayed, and I thanked God for Karen's life. We prayed for a smooth transition. We prayed for Karen's sister and daughter and son-in-law. I then encouraged Karen to lie back down, and I took the oil and anointed her. "Dear one, may the Lord bless you and keep you, may the Lord's face shine upon you and be gracious unto you, may the Lord look kindly upon you, and give you peace." I bent over and kissed her on the forehead.

"I love you," I said.

"I love you," she said.

We planned a transition service for my final Sunday at the Garden Church. I had an anxious knot in my stomach the entire week. The night before the service, David and I had dinner with Rev. Jane, our founding board chair and now the president of the Garden Church's denomination. "It's been a journey, hasn't it?" Jane said. I thanked her for her willingness to take a risk on this audacious idea, and for the many ways she had supported the work over the years.

Sunday morning, David and I drove over to pick up Sara, who had flown in from San Francisco for the day. "Honey, it's real," she said as we drove over the double bridges from Long Beach that spanned miles of port. "You planted a church."

When we all arrived at the church, my stomach clenched even tighter as I walked through the gates. After what felt like months of transition and saying goodbye, it was finally official transition day.

People scurried around getting ready, and my local clergy friends started coming through the gates. My heart warmed with each arrival. Rabbi Chuck from Temple Beth El appeared and gave me a big hug. "How you holding up?" he asked with a knowing look.

"Just barely," I replied, knowing that if I said more the tears would start. He squeezed my shoulder, and we changed the subject. All the clergy from the San Pedro Faith Consortium, a group we had founded over breakfasts at the Omelette and Waffle Shop, were there, along with my colleagues from Wayfarers Chapel, and other friends from the interfaith clergy community who had become friends. I suddenly felt less alone. They understood the comings and goings of clergy. They knew the pain of leaving a beloved congregation.

Rev. Amanda rang the gong to begin the service. Everything was a bit of a blur for me as I tried to focus on the parts of the liturgy that I was leading while also being present to the deep significance of the moment.

For the last time, I unpacked the tabernacle—this time with new objects I had gathered for the community. I blessed the new copy of the Bible, the candleholder specially selected for its ability to shelter the flame from the wind, the gong to call people together, the icon of the tree of life. As I lifted them up, we named the presence of God with us. Jedi listened from the side of the garden bed that curved around the sanctuary as Sara preached the sermon, recounting the stories of the Garden Church and its faithfulness in the past and her confidence in its faithfulness in the future. As Leia played at her grandma Linda's feet under the piano, I shared a brief message with them.

"Thank you for welcoming me into your town and your hearts and taking the risk with me to strive to create a sanctuary and a place to cultivate a more just and generous world," I said. I thanked them for believing in me when only five of us were at worship. I thanked them for helping me see the light of God in each person who came through the gates, even when some of those people interrupted the sermon again and again. I thanked them for changing my heart and letting theirs be changed as well. I thanked them for being one of the most beautiful expressions I'd ever seen of the kingdom of heaven.

I then shared a series of reminders: that this was God's table and everyone was welcome, even when the table was messy or complicated.

I looked out and saw a few people humming along as I said, "Remember that there is enough, enough and some to share, and that yes, everyone has something they are hungry for, but also, everyone has something to offer."

I reminded them about certain habits that churches can fall into. "Remember that things will be different in different seasons," I said. I reassured them that if they ever heard someone say, "Well, Reverend Anna always said we should . . ." they could respond, "And she also said that she knew things will continue to change—and that is good." I asked them to attend to God's guidance, since change is part of life and part of creation. God is always making all things new. A church is constantly called to reinvent itself, while staying faithful to its roots. "You *are* being the church," I declared. "You are doing it. You are it. You can do it. And it is beautiful."

I explained that everyone would receive a candle and a sprig of rosemary when they left that evening. A candle for the light, and rosemary for remembrance. "Remember you are loved," I said. "Remember to love others. Remember who you are together as a church. And remember to keep coming around God's table, where all are welcome to feed and to be fed, and look across for God's light in each other's eyes."

It was then time for our ritual of transition. Asher had served the Garden Church faithfully all fall, and his life was calling him out of the state, so Amanda and Jonathan were taking the mantle forward into the new year. Asher and I had written most of the liturgy, and he had beautifully crafted the words of transition as his gift to the congregation.

Jane, wearing the yellow and green stole that I had made for her when she was called as the denominational president, stood up to speak. "Reverend Anna," she said, "you were called by God and by the church to found the Garden Church and to serve the church that was yet to be born. You have answered this call for the past four years and you have served in this role faithfully."

Jane continued, witnessing to the journey of planting this church and the work of shepherding its growth. "As you go on to serve God, the church, and the world," she concluded, "we thank you and we give thanks to God for this new chapter in your journey and look forward to seeing the ways your ministry will continue forward."

I kept my eyes on her face as she spoke, and I tried to soak in what she was saying.

"Reverend Anna, as you continue in your ministry, will you continue in the work of reimagining church, and joyfully share the story of the Garden Church as evidence of God's continued work in the world, and will you continue to pray for the work of the Garden Church and Feed and Be Fed Farm?"

I smiled, looking out across the community, and replied that I would and that I would ask God to help me. That was easy. I couldn't imagine not holding this precious community in my heart and prayers. This story was one that was an honor to tell.

Jane continued, asking if I would entrust the Garden Church to God, to the people there, to the acting pastors and to the future leadership. Would I relinquish the office of pastor to this community?

I took a deep breath and replied, "I will, and I ask God to help me."

With those words, I felt a wave of grief and relief wash over me. God had called me to plant this church. I had done that. Now God was calling me to the next thing. This church was God's. And it would continue to be, without me. I felt peace and gratitude for the clear moment of delineation. This thing that I had been responsible for, prayed over, cried over, lain awake at night over, wracked in anxiety over, celebrated in great joy with, was no longer mine to hold. I relinquished it to the next leaders, to the people who were now a church, and to God, who had held it all along.

I had loved being part of that church. I loved our open gates and sanctuary, extending to the sky. I loved presiding over the table each week and looking into the eyes of so many people with so many different stories and reminding them—and being reminded myself—that we are beloved children of God. I loved being part of this big experiment and being a pastor to the neighborhood. I even loved weeding and watering, and I certainly loved taking fresh veggies home every day at the end of work. While I was well aware that God makes church everywhere, in all kinds of ways and places, it was hard for me to imagine that I would ever—could ever—find a place that I loved as deeply and fiercely as I did this community.

Jane prayed over me, over Jonathan and Amanda, and over the church as a whole. I took the new basket, the tabernacle, that I had gotten for them and handed it to Jonathan and Amanda. "Keep making church together," I said with tears in my eyes.

≈≈≈≈≈≈

A few days later, David and I drove down early for the Christmas Eve service so I could perform the one task that the new pastors had agreed I would do at this last service with them: set up the manger for baby Jesus and decorate it with flowers and herbs from the garden. I worked quietly, trying not to jump in to "correct" as people figured out where the light should go and how to transition a piece of the liturgy. A few times they turned and asked specific questions, but mostly I watched as they made it their own. After placing the last sprigs of rosemary and lavender around the head of the Christ child, David and I made our way to the coffee shop down the block. I sat in a booth near the window while David ordered our drinks.

I looked up from my phone to overhear Frank, whom we had just seen at the garden with his big backpack on, talking to David in an excited voice. "Look, look what I found in Jeremiah!" he said, pointing to the Spanish-language Bible in his hand. "It says, 'Plant gardens and eat their fruit . . . seek the peace of the city,'" he said, roughly translating Jeremiah 29:5, 7. "It's just what we're doing over at the Garden Church," he said, pointing excitedly at the Bible and then across the street.

David grinned and nodded. "Yes, indeed," he replied.

Jarrett came by a few minutes later, and Randy after him.

We sat and sipped our drinks and chatted with our neighbors and friends. "It's amazing, honey," I said to David. "This is the same booth I sat at when I first found 6th Street on that first scouting trip, wondering if this could be the place to plant this church. And here we are."

We walked back to church and slipped in near the back. Communion came around and Jonathan served me the bread and Tim served me the cup with a knowing smile. As long as they keep breaking bread and sharing it, I thought, all will be well. God is here.

Later that evening, David and I settled on the air mattress in Nora's entryway and Asher curled up on the couch in the living room—a full little home and family to spend Christmas with. On Christmas morning we made breakfast, opened stockings, had family worship, and exchanged presents before heading over to Connie and Tim's to spend the rest of the day with their family.

Connie and Tim gave me three perfect gifts. An engaging book of short stories that I could read and be distracted by, but also be fed. A little string of lights reminiscent of the ones we use at church, but to be hung indoors. And then, my favorite gift, a shepherd's staff. "For the reverend to wrangle her sheep, wherever and whoever they are," Tim said. He had found it at an antique store and sanded it and varnished it. A new favorite possession.

Connie took us on a long walk through the ravine behind their home, and we spent time sitting on a bench wondering at nature and God with us. When we got back, Tim had the pizza oven hot. We made and ate homemade pizzas, and then made a bunch more to cut and wrap up and take to our neighbors on the streets.

We went down to Kurt's Kitchen, the Catholic Worker house that serves dinner every Monday and Tuesday night. Connie said she had just seen Betty leave. Asher, David, and I went out to look for her. We didn't find her at first, but we did find Jimmy. He was happy and surprised to see us.

"I thought you'd be on your way to New York by now," he said.

"Not quite—tomorrow," I replied. He told us how his Christmas was wonderful because he had gotten to go to a friend's house and take a shower.

"First time in eight months," he said. "You have no idea how dirty I was. I always try to get cleaned up in the sink, but it's just not the same as a shower. And the cops keep kicking me out of the bathroom. I know some people are in there doing bad stuff, but I'm just trying to get clean." We offered him socks, but he said he had lots of them. And even some new shoes. "I'm not wearing them yet, I'm saving them. They were a gift. But man, the best gift was that shower."

We walked back to Kurt's Kitchen and found Betty out front. She hadn't been to church for weeks and had been unresponsive when people had seen her on the street. She was tying something to her cart as I walked up. "Betty! I'm so glad to see you!" I said. She looked up and a flash of recognition went across her face. "Can I give you a hug?" I asked.

"No, no, thank you, that won't be necessary," she replied.

"Know that we love you and miss you," I said. She looked down, but seemed to be listening as she finished tying the item onto her cart and began to walk away.

We took our bags of coats, hats, and socks, and our home-made pizza, and started walking around the block. We didn't have to go far—there were camps everywhere. The first group was glad for the pizza, but didn't really want socks. The next group had just eaten pizza, but was very interested in scarves and gloves. "Oh wait, I know you—you're from the Garden Church," one man said. They offered us muffins, which Connie graciously took and ate. At the next camp a man didn't want any food or clothing, but thanked us for coming out.

"It's people like you—people who actually see us—that we need here."

Then a woman popped her head out of the tent. "Wait, do you have any coats?" One of Connie's sons took one over to her.

We kept walking. A yappy dog was guarding the next encampment. A man who was deaf refused the thing he could not hear us offering, then gladly gobbled up two pieces of pizza after he saw them. A woman happily took the last scarf and pizza and socks. We only had a few things left as we started back to the cars. "We should sing!" I said, and Nora started us off on "O Come, All Ye Faithful."

When we got to the cars Connie said, "So is this it? Goodbye for now?"

"I think so," I replied. We hugged. I couldn't think of a better way to end my time in San Pedro than walking around the neighborhood and being with all our neighbors.

The next day, after a tearful goodbye with Nora, David and I drove our little purple Honda, loaded with the rest of my things, down to the church. I had pulled up the photo I'd taken in February 2014 when sitting outside on the street, looking in the gates, and wondering if that was *the* church. Then I took a matching one, marveling at all that had happened since that first time I'd laid eyes on the lot.

David and I stood by the gates. I anointed them once more.

"With gratitude for all that has been," I said, "for courage and protection, for provision and abundance, for all that emanates out from God's table to continue to do so, for everyone who walks through the gates to be seen as who they are, precious children of God."

It was peaceful and quiet on the street. I didn't go in. I was ready to say goodbye. I went back to the car to post the two photos and my words of gratitude online, while David walked up to the coffee shop to get us drinks for the road. Katie and her boyfriend walked by, and I watched as they paused at the gate and offered a quiet prayer as they went on their way. David returned and we stared together at the gates for a few minutes.

"It's an amazing thing you've done here, Anna," he said.

"Me and God and a whole bunch of people," I replied. "It's a church," I said between tears. "It's a church that's a garden and a garden that's a church. And it is good."

EPILOGUE

I am writing this epilogue as I sit in the neighborhood coffee shop in Gambier, Ohio, where most of this book has been written. I have just taken a break from packing boxes in our apartment around the corner. Since that day we drove away from the gates, my journey with David has taken us to upstate New York, then to Ohio for a year, and now we are heading to Massachusetts. As we have made a life together, we have had joys and losses, and we continually take comfort in the God who goes with us.

As I packed up my office this morning, the tabernacle objects of the Garden Church that still live with me were packed up too. The canvas-covered Bible, with the juice stains and dirt smudges, was recently used for a seminary class I taught. It went into the box. I packed up the candle that sits on my desk. When I am on the phone doing work as a consultant, I light it to remember the wisdom of the Holy Spirit. The gong, too, was carefully wrapped in a large scarf and set aside to take to a conference next week.

I left the Garden Church, but its story continued. It is, in fact, alive and well today. But that story is for others to tell. I do get snapshots on occasion. Rev. Jonathan emailed to say they had baptized one of our unhoused neighbors. Rev. Amanda called to discuss some of our original intentions and also wondered about funding strategies and staffing models. Connie texted to share that when Jedi got back from his first year of college, he went straight to the Garden Church with a big bag of nonperishable food for the church that he had bought with the remainder of his school meal card money. Occasionally one of them will send me a photo, the most recent one being Dino all dressed up for the church's birthday party.

Throughout my journey with the Garden Church, a prominent image in the Swedenborgian tradition kept returning to me: the vision at the end of the Book of Revelation of a heavenly city, the New Jerusalem, descending out of heaven. This city is a picture of a more heavenly way of being, here and now on earth. In this picture, the church, in the big, universal sense of the word, is a place where all different kinds of people come together, through all twelve gates of the city, all different types of religious paths. It is a place where there is no temple to God, because God is everywhere. In the middle is the tree of life. The tree that we see at the beginning of the Bible in the garden of Eden reappears here, with its twelve kinds of fruit, one for each month—all kinds of food for all kinds of people, and leaves that will heal the nations. The image nurtures a fertile soil where unique gifts can grow and make us whole rather than divide. The tree of life brings together something that feels impossible in this world: different types of fruit all on the same tree. The richness of many branches of the family in one space, unique offerings honoring all who come around the table.

And this is what I found, in its messy and beautiful way, in the Garden Church. People from all different backgrounds could find belonging and bring their various experiences together to be church. It was a church that grew out of and was supported by a particular tradition, yet was from its founding nurtured by people across traditions and people with no tradition at all. What we had in common was this: we were all part of this tree of life and we were all being drawn together around God's table, a table at which we could serve and boldly proclaim God's welcome, God's table where all are welcome, to feed and to be fed.

A building is not what makes a church. The heavenly city has no temple. Being there for fifty or five hundred years is not what makes a church. The Garden Church brought into focus the power and the essence of church, as people gathered together to love God and love neighbor, share in the sacraments, belong to one another, and serve together. Rooted in the rich gifts of the faithful who have come before, we found the body of Christ together in the garden. We came together around the table believing that we were being nourished in the same stream of the water of life. Yes, there are all sorts of imperfections and struggles; yes, God is still breathing life and love into her church as we come together to be church beyond the walls.

My time with the Garden Church is not a story of permanence or arrival. The Garden Church taught me this: God is making church all over the place, beyond the walls, on the streets, in the soil, and around the table. Whenever we gather together, God is with us. Wherever we pitch our tents, she will pitch hers too.

ACKNOWLEDGMENTS

Church planting and writing a book have in common the fluctuation between the feeling that you're doing it all on your own, and the truth that it is a community effort. In thanking those who have been part of making this book possible, I must start with those who helped bring the Garden Church into being.

Thank you to the people of the New Church of Boulder Valley, who welcomed me into their midst, trusted me to lead and care for them, and will forever be the first church that captured my heart. And thank you to David Roth for your friendship and colleagueship throughout the years. Thank you to my seminary professors at Earlham School of Religion, Bethany Theological Seminary, and the Swedenborgian House of Studies, in particular Dawn Ottoni-Wilhelm, Scott Holland, David Johns, Jim Lawrence, Devin Zuber, and my classmates who taught me and explored with me.

Thank you to church planter friends David Roth, Frank Rose, Emily Scott, Nadia Bolz-Weber, Kerlin Richter, Ethan McCardell, Mac Frazier, and Grant Schnarr. You showed me it could be done and shared the niche outlook on church that bonds church planters together. And thank you to Bronwen Mayer Henry for her constant colleagueship and friendship along the way.

I am grateful to the Center for Swedenborgian Studies, the Swedenborgian Church of North America, the Pacific Coast Association, and Wayfarers Chapel, for embracing what could be, taking a risk, and supporting a new ministry. Particular thanks to Jim Lawrence, Jane Siebert, Rachel Rivers, Robert Carr, and Dave Brown.

Thank you to St. Gregory of Nyssa Episcopal Church, the Food Pantry—especially Sara Miles, Paul Fromberg, Sylvia Miller-Mutia, and Sanford Dole, who gave this unknown seminary student a chance and welcomed me onto the team. You introduced me to a Jesus I didn't even know I was missing, showed me what happens when all are welcome "without exception," and were the best big-sister church and cheering squad a church planter could ask for.

Thank you to the start-up board of directors of the Garden Church: Katharine Carr, Jana Carter, Rebecca Esterson, Jennifer Lindsay, Emma Ogley-Oliver, Amy Gall Ritchie, and Jane Siebert, who took a risk, believed in a dream, and rode the roller coaster with faith, curiosity, and generosity. Thank you to those locally who were with us from the very beginning and helped form and inform what would be, especially Christine, Cory, Dana, Janice, Juho, Karen, Lara, Lori, Nancy, Rachel, and Scott. Thank you also to the board members and leadership team members who joined in the work over the years: Nigel

Brown, Annette Ciketic, Rudy Caseres, Yancy Deron, Jedidiah Fite, TeaJ Johnson, Lara Hughey, Jonathan Mitchell, Connie McOsker, Linda O'Brien, Asher O'Callaghan, Bree Proffitt, Ebony Perry, Nancy Richardson, Peter Rothe, Sarah Rothe, Ed Ruiz, Windy, Osmara Reyes-Osorio, Amanda Adams Riley, Connor Thompson, Nora Woofenden, and Octavia Wright. And to Tim McOsker for his wisdom and support.

I am grateful to the Garden Church cultivation team, made up of over two hundred people across the world, who prayed, pledged, and shared the vision of the Garden Church when nary a tomato had been planted. I am grateful to all the members of the early prayer team for witnessing the vision and believing it into being with me.

Thanks to Fred Dunlap, who told me twelve years prior that when I started a church he wanted to support it. Thanks to the two angel donors at whose kitchen table I burst into tears, wondering if we would be able to continue, and to those who came along just when we needed you and gave with a generosity that brought me to tears all over again. To the churches and associations that gave, particularly Wayfarers Chapel, San Francisco Swedenborgian Church, the New York Korean Swedenborgian Church, the Ohio Association, and the Pacific Coast Association. To friends, relatives, professors, and colleagues who gave generously, supporting something from which they would never directly benefit. Your generosity continues to humble and inspire me. You know who you are. I am grateful.

I particularly want to honor three saints who are no longer alive in this realm but who are imprinted on the life of the church. Karen Kessler, a founding member of the Garden Church, who was consistent in her prayers and support in so many ways; Elizabeth Boileau from Saint Gregory's, who showed me what it looked like to feed faithfully; and Grandma Shirley Gladish, who prayed consistently, was always curious about and supportive of the work, and who believed in it from the start.

Thank you to Lara Hughey, Scott Anger, Bree Aseltine Proffitt, Holly Howard, Quia Anderson, and Christine Wamba, each of whom served as a part of the Garden Church team in various capacities and shaped this work with your gifts and contributions. Thank you to Trish Pottersmith, who gave hundreds of volunteer hours from the very beginning to do all of our tech and website, cheered and supported constantly, and who was one of our most involved "from afar" members. And thank you to Nora Woofenden, who was there through every step, as a musician, a generous volunteer, and, most dear to me, as my sister.

Thank you to the many people of the Garden Church. I fear even beginning to name you because I will miss someone and you are all precious. I pray this story honors you and the gifts you each bring to the church and the world. I am honored to have been your pastor. Thank you to the San Pedro community for being the fertile soil in which to plant and for embracing the Garden Church as part of your community.

Thank you to my clergy colleagues in southern California: to those who supported the early years, especially Rev. Sean Lanigan, Joel Bergeland, Jonipher Kupono Kwong, Dave Brown, and the staff at Wayfarers Chapel. Thank you to my dear San Pedro Faith Consortium co-conspirators, Pastor Lisa Williams, Rabbi Chuck Briskin, and Revs. Jeanette Repp and Neal Neuenschwander for the many breakfasts at Omelette and Waffle Shop and the conversations, actions, and prayers that we shared together.

Thank you to my colleagues from afar, especially Revs. Sarah Buteux, Sage Cole, Carol Howard Merritt, Paul Fromberg, Nadia Bolz-Weber, Ben Johnston-Krase, and Amy Gall Ritchie. Your calls, texts, advice, and prayers kept me going. I am grateful for the many conversations with Kendall Vanderslice, Fred Bahnson, Heber Brown, Nurya Love Parish, John Senior, Sam Chamelin and so many others who are working at the intersection of food and faith. Thank you to my beloveds in the Sexy Dangerous Preachers Cohort: Revs. Asher O'Callaghan, Gemma Sampson, Alex Darling-Raabe, Sylvia Miller-Mutia, Kerri Meyer, Reagan Humber, Amy Hanson, and Lauren Lukason. Wrestling with Scripture and life with you, your swears and prayers, are forever a gift. Thank you to my mentors Sara Miles and Rachel Rivers, and to my spiritual directors Emma Churchman, Amy Gall Ritchie, and Sister Julia Costello: you kept me afloat and pointed me back to God and God's people. And thank you to my coach and wise guide, Martha Pitcairn, who keeps showing up to witness the journey.

Rev. Dr. Amanda Riley and Rev. Dr. Jonathan Mitchell: I am beyond grateful that God called the two of you to be the Garden Church's next pastors and celebrate the incredible ministry you both bring. It was hard to imagine handing the leadership of this baby church over to someone else, yet you made it imaginable. Thank you.

Writing the story of the Garden Church has called me into admitting I'm a writer. My thanks go to Pat DeWitt Thomas, Amy Lyles Wilson, and Carol Howard Merritt for telling me it was true many years ago. This book would not be here without the wisdom, encouragement, and annoying persistence of Sara Miles, who told me before we'd even found the lot at 6th

Street that I would need to write a book about it. She asked me to write her messy field notes most weeks. Without that encouragement and those emailed stories and fragments of conversation, this book would not be what it is today. Without Sara's modeling, mentorship, faith, and friendship, I would not be who I am today.

My writing communities continue to encourage me and teach me. Thank you to the Speaking of Writing group: your wisdom and experiences are gold and I'm humbled to be amongst you. Thank you to the Grammatical Foibles writing group: you have given feedback, edited, prayed, cried, sent my butt back to my chair, and sent boxes of snacks and a "nevertheless she persisted" necklace to keep me there. Thank you to Jana Riess for your encouragement and professional advice (along with your precious friendship and forever revered role as Wise Matchmaker). Thank you to Joy Brennon, my writing accountability buddy in Gambier. Thank you to the beta readers who took the time, energy, and thought to read and comment on the manuscript. Your questions and highlights and ideas helped me to look at this book through fresh eyes. Thank you to Rebecca Esterson, Hilary Floyd, and Megan Westra for your expertise in Hebrew and Greek and for helping me to understand what I was trying to say.

To my dad, Ian Woofenden, for his hours upon hours of editing, from early proposal drafts to the very end. He has given his critical eye and proud support throughout the process. Thank you to Skye Kerr Levy, my development editor, whose ability to shape a sentence is equal to her deep insight. She invited me to dig more deeply into my own experiences and become an author. Thank you for being there every step of the journey and assuring me in words and practice that I wasn't alone.

Thank you to Katherine Willis Pershey for introducing me to the good people at Herald Press. To Valerie Weaver-Zercher for listening to my pitch even in the "last day of the conference exhaustion," for *getting* the heart of this book, and for wisely and patiently walking me through the process. To Sara Versluis, who stepped in and took the editor baton to the finish line. Thank you for your literary and human wisdom, for pulling me forward, and for recognizing and honoring the story. Thank you to the rest of the team at Herald Press and MennoMedia, executive director and publisher Amy Gingerich and the graphic designers and marketing team, for caring about the birth of this book at every stage.

Thank you to Wiggin Street Coffee in Gambier, Ohio, where much of this book was written. And thank you to the Gambier and Kenyon College community members, who offered encouragement by stopping by or by seeing my earphones in and waving from a distance. Particular thanks to Elizabeth Dark and Rachel, Leeman, Amanda, and Martin Kessler. You don't know how often the greeting of a fiery five-year-old reporting on her new bike or the impish grin of a toddler was just the thing this writer needed to keep going. And to Jess Kotnour for wanting to hear the story and for sharing your hunger for what the church can be.

Thank you to my posse: Athena, Rose, Nora, Claire, Susan, Linda, Debbie, Jana, Rebecca, Bronwen, and Julie. You have stood with me throughout my life, you stood at our wedding, and you stand with me still. I am the luckiest.

Thank you to my family by birth, choice, and marriage: Woofendens, Gladishs, Cohen-Glebes, Roths, Abelkis, Reuters,

Howletts, and Smiths. I love you all and am grateful to call you family. Special thanks to the children in these families who call me to work for a world that you deserve to grow up in.

Thank you to my grandparents: Shirley and Dave Gladish, and Louise and Bill Woofenden. Your writing, love, and lives of faith inspire me. I wish you were still here to read this story.

Thank you to my parents, Frea Gladish and Ian Woofenden, who raised me in close proximity to dirt and plants and who encouraged me and gave me space to experiment and explore when I came to them saying, "I have the best new idea!" and who love and encourage me still.

And thank you to my husband, David, who wasn't scared away when Jana introduced us and told him I was a pastor. His appreciation of and involvement in the Garden Church made me love him even more. He has supported this book from beginning to end. He is the partner who was well worth waiting for. I am so glad to be living life with him. Dearest: life is better with you.

nōTes

CHAPTER 1

1 "'Nones' on the Rise," Pew Research Center, October 9, 2012, https://www.pewforum.org/2012/10/09/nones-on-the-rise/.

CHAPTER 2

1 Kendell Vanderslice, "Reverend Dr. Heber Brown and the Black Church Food Security Network," Good Food Jobs, October 9, 2018, https://www.goodfoodjobs.com/blog/reverend-dr-heber-brown-and-the-black-church-food-security-network/.

CHAPTER 3

1 James Alison, *Broken Hearts and New Creations: Intimations of a Great Reversal* (London: Continuum, 2010), 165, quoted in Brian McLaren, *Why Did Jesus, Moses, the Buddha, and Mohammed Cross the Road? Christian Identity in a Multi-faith World* (New York: Jericho Books, 2012), 13.

CHAPTER 4

1 Rozella Haydée White, *Love Big: The Power of Revolutionary Relationships to Heal the World* (Minneapolis: Augsburg Books, 2019), 12.

2 Kerri Meyer, conversation with author, September 25, 2016.

CHAPTER 5

1 Nikki Cooley, interview with Ryan Heinsius, "Bearing Witness: Voices of Climate Change Part VII: Adapting Tribal Ceremonies To A Changing Climate," Knau, accessed June 16, 2019, https://www.knau.org/post/bearing-witness-voices-climate-change-part-vii-adapting-tribal-ceremonies-changing-climate.

2 *The Inclusive Bible: The First Egalitarian Translation* (Lanham, MD: Rowman and Littlefield, 2007), 697.

3 Madeleine L'Engle, *Walking on Water: Reflections on Faith and Art* (New York: North Point Press, 1980), 50.

4 Diana Butler Bass, *Grounded* (San Francisco: HarperOne, 2017).

5 "'Nones' on the Rise," Pew Research Center, October 9, 2012, https://www.pewforum.org/2012/10/09/nones-on-the-rise/.

CHAPTER 6

1 I am indebted to the work of John Senior, who presented his manuscript, "Liberating Circulatory Power: Two Case Studies from Food Justice Movements," at the 2018 American Academy of Religion meeting in Denver, Colorado, and is the source of the ideas discussed here.

2 John Senior, "Liberating Circulatory Power: Two Case Studies from Food Justice Movements" (unpublished manuscript), November 18, 2018, PDF.

3 For more on watershed discipleship and the Wild Church Network, see https://watersheddiscipleship.org/ and https://www.wildchurchnetwork.com/.

CHAPTER 7

1 Thomas Merton, *Conjectures of a Guilty Bystander* (New York: Image Books, 1966), 53.

2 "Reducing the Impact of Wasted Food by Feeding the Soil and Composting," EPA, last modified August 2, 2018, https://www.epa.gov/sustainable-management-food/reducing-impact-wasted-food-feeding-soil-and-composting.

CHAPTER 8

1 Helen Keller, *My Religion* (West Chester, PA: The Swedenborg Foundation, 1960), 115. First published 1927.

2 "A Moral Agenda Based on Fundamental Rights," Poor People's Campaign, accessed June 1, 2019, https://www.poorpeoples campaign.org/demands/.

3 Cornel West, Twitter post, February 14, 2017, 8:15 p.m., https://twitter.com/cornelwest/status/831718432995319808.

CHAPTER 9

1 Sheldon W. Sorge, *Feasting on the Word: Preaching the Revised Common Lectionary*, Vol. 2, ed. David L. Bartlett and Barbara Brown Taylor (Louisville: Westminster John Knox Press, 2009), 270.

2 Paul Fromberg and Sara Miles, "Eucharististic Prayer," Saint Gregory's, accessed June 1, 2019, https://www.saintgregorys.org/uploads/2/4/2/6/24265184/eucharistic_prayer_with_intercessions_mdg.pdf.

3 Ibid.

4 Rachel Held Evans, *Searching for Sunday: Loving, Leaving, and Finding the Church* (Nashville: Nelson Books, 2015), 148.

5 Kendall Vanderslice, *We Will Feast: Rethinking Dinner, Worship, and the Community of God* (Grand Rapids: Erdmans, 2019), 3.

CHAPTER 11

1 The Iona Community, comp., *Iona Abbey Worship Book* (Glasgow: Wild Goose Publications, 2001), 115.

2 St. Gregory of Nyssa Episcopal Church, San Francisco, California, vigil liturgy 2019.

3 John Chrysostom, "Paschal Sermon," excerpted from "Easter Vigil 2016," St. Gregory of Nyssa Episcopal Church, March 26, 2016, https://www.saintgregorys.org/uploads/2/4/2/6/24265184/vigil_script_2016.pdf.

4 This and following quotations are from Sara Miles, sermon, April 16, 2017, Garden Church, San Pedro, California. Used with permission.

CHAPTER 12

1 Shirley Erena Murray, "For Everyone Born, a Place at the Table" (Carol Stream, IL: Hope Publishing Company, 1998).

2 Emanuel Swedenborg, *Secrets of Heaven* vol. 2, trans. Lisa Hyatt Cooper, §1799:4 (West Chester, PA: Swedenborg Foundation, 2013).

THE AUTHOR

Anna Woofenden is a writer, speaker, pastor, and leading voice in the food and faith movement. She is the founding pastor of the Garden Church in San Pedro, California, founder of Feed and Be Fed Farm, and cohost of the *Food and Faith* podcast. She serves as the Protestant chaplain at Amherst College and lives with her husband, David, in Northampton, Massachusetts. Woofenden is passionate about spirituality, justice, food, the earth, and community, and is driven by a calling to reimagine church. Connect with her at AnnaWoofenden.com.

CPSIA information can be obtained
at www.ICGtesting.com
Printed in the USA
LVHW042045090420
652873LV00001B/1